Presented to:

_____

By:

_____

Date:

_____

ZONDERVAN

The Beautiful Word Devotional

Copyright © 2017 by Zondervan

Published in Grand Rapids, Michigan, by Zondervan. Zondervan is a registered trademark of The Zondervan Corporation, L.L.C., a wholly owned subsidiary of HarperCollins Christian Publishing, Inc.

Requests for information should be addressed to customercare@harpercollins.com.

ISBN 978-0-7180-8849-1 (HC)
ISBN 978-0-7180-8661-9 (eBook)

Cover design: Katie Jennings Design

Cover illustration: Mia Charro

Interior illustration: Kerri Charlton, Tiffany Zajas, Micah Kandros Design, Connie Gabbert Design and Illustration, Jasmine Jones, and Jay and Kristi Smith of Juicebox Designs

Interior design: Lori Lynch

Printed in Malaysia

24 25 26 27 28 OFF 13 12 11 10 9

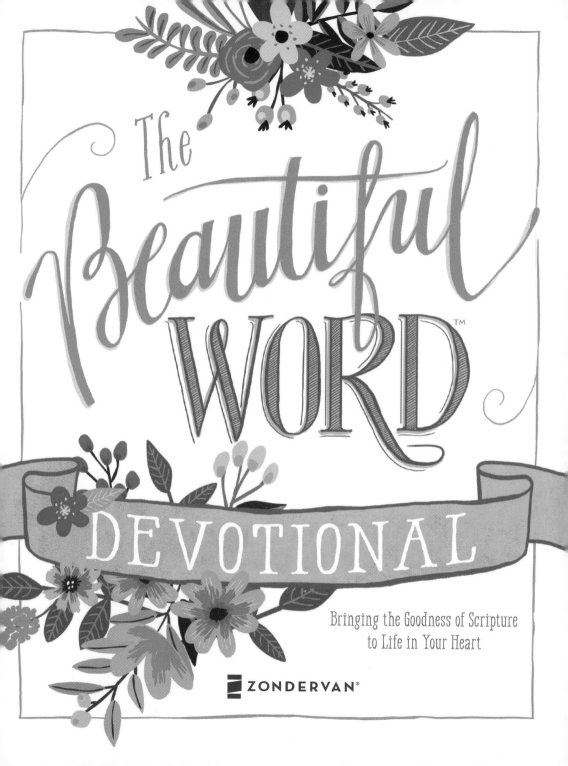

The Beautiful Word™

WORD

DEVOTIONAL

Bringing the Goodness of Scripture
to Life in Your Heart

ZONDERVAN®

January

*Then God said, "Let us make mankind
in our image, in our likeness."*

GENESIS 1:26

God created you to be in relationship—and that simple truth will transform your life.

In fact, God himself is a relationship, a three-party relationship (Father, Son, and Holy Spirit) that expressed its joy by creating you! And you're made in his likeness, which means you are worthy, dignified, and beautiful.

God created you to have significant relationships with others. Scripture shows he made Eve because Adam was alone. After that they enjoyed the first human relationship, working and laughing alongside each other.

God also created you to be in a life-enhancing relationship with him. He fashioned you so that you would walk with him, share your struggles with him, and follow after him. You'll never outgrow your need for him, and he'll never run away from you. He is that constant, steady friend.

*Lord, thanks for creating me worthy. Help
me to choose to be near you, amen.*

*See what great love the Father has lavished on
us, that we should be called children of God!*

1 JOHN 3:1

A long time ago roller skates were not
smooth riding like they are today. They
used to be metal-wheeled contraptions that
clamped onto your tennis shoes. If you were
lucky enough (depending on your attitude
toward fire), sparks would fly from the wheels
as you bumped along.

Thinking about roller skates reminds me
about childhood—a time of freedom, creativity, and belonging. Some of us have smooth
memories—of laughter and joy. Others have
metal-contraption memories—of rough riding
and unwanted sparks.

Regardless of your childhood, whether you
were well loved by your parents or even abandoned, the truth still remains: you are loved.
The God who created you, who fashioned you
in your mother's womb, cheers for you and
loves you with abandon. If that's hard to comprehend, it's okay. Your feelings do not alter
the bedrock truth of God's lavish love.

*Lord, it's hard to fathom that you
actually love me, that you call me your
beloved child. Help me to live in light of
that beautiful truth today, amen.*

*Wisdom is more precious than rubies, and
nothing you desire can compare with her.*

PROVERBS 8:11

Our consumer culture thrives on desire. An advertiser's main objective is to make you want something, to get you to the place where you truly believe that a certain item will fully satisfy you and change your life for the better. *That new jacket will make me feel better about myself. That house will totally improve my life. That school will ensure my child gets into a better college.*

The problem is this: God made your heart for him, not for stuff. Nothing will satisfy you the way he will. When you choose to follow him, not only do you gain a healthy sense of self-worth, but you also receive something else truly important—wisdom.

Wisdom helps you make positive choices throughout the day. It enables you to discern between truth and lies. It gives you the ability to read people better. And wisdom provides peace as you make bigger decisions. Chase after God's wisdom, and you will find life that is truly abundant. And as God provides that wisdom, you'll find you won't need to chase after things.

*Lord, help me chase wisdom—
and you—today, amen.*

January 4

The eyes of the Lord are on the righteous and his ears are attentive to their prayer, but the face of the Lord is against those who do evil.

1 PETER 3:12

Most people use their vision and hearing every day. We see a budding rose. We hear children's laughter. Through these two important senses, we experience much of life.

Isn't it amazing that God exercises these same senses in relation to you?

He sees you—even the sides of you no one else sees. He takes notice of the sacrifices you make, the longings of your heart, the hope you hold way deep inside.

He listens to you and hears the groans that accompany a painful loss, the songs you belt out in the car as you run errands, the words of affirmation you speak to your children. And when you pray, oh, how he listens. Scripture says he is attentive to your prayer. Picture God leaning in.

This truth is a tremendous encouragement! You are seen! You are heard! Rest in that today.

Lord, I am grateful today that you see me, every part of me, and you hear me, every prayer I pray. Thank you, amen.

*"Do to others as you would
have them do to you."*

LUKE 6:31

Such a simple statement, but so profound. Even people who don't yet know Jesus know this golden rule. Why? Because it's a great basic guideline for life. Furthermore, everyone longs to be loved this way. We thrive when others love us the way they care for themselves.

In our culture of hyper self-centeredness, this kind of love utterly stands out. When you choose to love people as you would love to be loved, the world takes notice. After all, this kind of love doesn't involve platitudes or clichés. No, this kind of love takes action.

If you would love to be thanked, thank others. If you would like to be forgiven by someone, forgive those you need to forgive. If you would love a word of encouragement, encourage someone today.

In short, give what you would like to receive. Doing so will change not only your life, but also the lives of those whom you love with your actions.

*Lord, show me someone today whom I could
love in a way I would like to be loved, amen.*

January 6

*You know the grace of our Lord Jesus
Christ, that though he was rich, yet for
your sake he became poor, so that you
through his poverty might become rich.*

2 CORINTHIANS 8:9

*I*magine being one of the world's billionaires. Anything you wanted you could have. And then imagine giving it all up for the sake of your child because an evil genius has kidnapped him or her and demanded your fortune.

People trump riches. Human beings are priceless and irreplaceable. This is why Jesus Christ, who ruled in heaven undoubtedly with riches and glory aplenty, chose to leave all that splendor and enter into our dirt-stained world. Because he sees us as worth fighting for.

Jesus gave up wealth. He became poor so that he could make a way for you to be in a rich, life-giving relationship with him. His choice of poverty opened up a treasure trove of wealth for you—a life rich in purpose and hope and grace and power. Your Savior sacrificed all that for you—his child whom he deeply loves.

*Lord, I am stunned by your love for
me. Thank you for leaving heaven to
rescue me from the consequences of my
sin and a meaningless life, amen.*

*Let us not love with words or speech
but with actions and in truth.*

1 JOHN 3:18

It's easy to say the right words, the words that people want to hear. It's harder to live out the meaning of those words. As the apostle John taught, we need to demonstrate our love: rather than merely talking about our love, we are to love "with actions and in truth."

When we love "with actions," we show others we love them. When our spouse is exhausted, we do the dishes. When our friend is hurting, we send flowers. When a child is sick, we help her through a feverish night.

When we love someone "in truth," we are also willing to tell them truth they may not want to hear. We lovingly tell a friend we're worried about her drinking. We love relatives by gently telling the truth about the past. Then, when our friend is amazing, we give specific positive feedback.

What will you do to love someone "in truth" today? Whom will you love with actions—and what will those actions be?

*Lord, teach me to show my love to
the people in my life with my actions,
not just the words I say, amen.*

January 8

*"Seek first his kingdom and his righteousness,
and all these things will be given to you as well."*

MATTHEW 6:33

These aren't the only comforting yet challenging words Jesus spoke in his Sermon on the Mount. Jesus had more: Don't go after everything you want. Don't build your own empire or kingdom. Don't live in isolation or by your own strength. Don't run after money or possessions or fame, making them idols.

Instead, Jesus encouraged his followers to seek his kingdom and his righteousness. When our focus is on God and obedience to his commands, as well as loving him and others, he will provide the food and clothing he knows we need. Pursue things, and you get them plus emptiness. Pursue God, and you receive him—and joy, peace, love, and much more—plus all you need in this life. .

Are you tired of chasing after things that don't satisfy? Or have you fulfilled a long-held dream, yet feel empty? Spend time with God today, telling him of your emptiness, giving him your worries, and asking him to show you how to seek his kingdom first.

*Lord, teach me to seek you and
your kingdom first, amen.*

"For my thoughts are not your thoughts, neither are your ways my ways." ISAIAH 55:8

"For my thoughts are not your thoughts, neither are your ways my ways," declares the LORD.

ISAIAH 55:8

Imagine a tiny point and let it represent your mind. God's mind is like the line that extends from that dot into forever. The almighty God is bigger than the universe he created, more powerful than the Pacific Ocean, more magnificent than the Grand Canyon, and higher than Everest.

This truth may make you feel small, but at the same time you may experience deep reassurance. After all, the God who is immeasurable and unfathomable loves you and longs to have a relationship with you.

At times you will doubt. When life careens out of control, you may be tempted to think you would do a better job running the universe. In those moments, remember Isaiah 55:8. In God's hands, today's catastrophe becomes tomorrow's testimony. That loss you're grieving will always be hard to think about, but you'll emerge with more empathy for others, and a greater awe for God whose mysterious ways are definitely different from ours.

Lord, I confess that I don't know how to run this world or even my own world. Help me to rely on you, the One whose thoughts are far greater than mine, amen.

January 10

*Jesus said to her, "I am the resurrection
and the life. The one who believes in
me will live, even though they die."*

JOHN 11:25

*E*very single one of us will die—but in today's
verse Jesus promises something extraordinary. Our faith in the truth that he has
risen from the dead means that we will be resurrected as well! This is not an idle promise. It
is backed by the death he experienced on the
cross and his glorious resurrection.

The choice is yours today. The passage-
way to eternal life is plain, unadorned belief
that what God says is actually true: his Son—
who was without sin—took the punishment
we deserved for our sin, died on the cross, and
was raised from the dead.

Jesus is the resurrection—*your* resurrection
—and the life—*your* life abundant while you
are on this earth and then life eternal with him.
He will give you joy to face trials, and one day
he will usher you into heaven.

*Lord, my faith in you and my relationship
with you give me new life now and
life eternal. Thank you, amen.*

The LORD your GOD is with YOU, the mighty WARRIOR who SAVES. Zephaniah 3:17

"The LORD your God is with you, the Mighty Warrior who saves. He will take great delight in you; in his love he will no longer rebuke you, but will rejoice over you with singing."

ZEPHANIAH 3:17

When a baby is fussy, tossing and turning, unable to fall asleep, one thing a mother has in her arsenal of tricks is simply her voice. She enters the room, pats her sweet baby on the back, and sings soothing songs over the restless infant.

Imagine that picture for a moment. You are tossing a worry around in your head over and over again. Perhaps you can't sleep from all the competing fears. That's when you need to take a deep breath and choose to believe the truth of Zephaniah 3:17. God will sing over you. As you turn to him in your restlessness, he will sing songs over you of deliverance, hope, and peace just as a good mother sings over her fussy child.

Lord, help me to slow down and trust that you are singing over me as you handle my worries today, amen.

"Whoever can be trusted with very little can also be trusted with much, and whoever is dishonest with very little will also be dishonest with much."

LUKE 16:10

*L*ittle children enjoy making mud pies. They will practice their "art" with mud before their parents open up the kitchen to them. This is a small example of learning to be faithful in a small thing (mud) before we can be entrusted with big things (actual cakes).

God entrusts you with bigger and bigger things the more you are faithful in the smaller and even unseen things. How you handle your money, for instance, reveals your character. Whether you manage a household budget or a multimillion-dollar account, your integrity matters.

You may feel like your sphere of influence is small, but what you do in these smaller spaces (making and keeping to a budget, running a home, being a good employee) reveals your heart. Strive to be faithful when you're unnoticed, and as you are, people will take notice. More importantly, God will see, and he will entrust you with more responsibility in his kingdom.

Lord, help me be faithful in the small things so that you will choose to trust me with bigger things, amen.

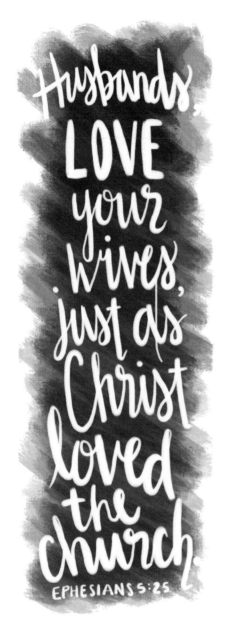

EPHESIANS 5:25

Husbands, love your wives, just as Christ loved the church and gave himself up for her.

EPHESIANS 5:25

You may think this verse doesn't apply to you if you're not a husband. But this verse about sacrificial love reminds all of us how every relationship should work. If we want to love well, we must love like Jesus did.

And how did Jesus love? He gave up his life, his will, his desires—all for the sake of others. He did not come to be served but to serve others and give up his life for our sins. That kind of sacrificial love should pervade every part of our lives.

And we don't have to try to love that way on our own. When we meet Jesus, the Holy Spirit enters into our lives, and he enables us to love like that. We can't muster up that kind of love on our own, although we do have a choice in the matter. We choose to learn the art of relying on the Spirit's promptings about whom and how to love. And when he prompts, we act.

Lord, may my love for others reflect the kind of love you've shown me. I want to love like you do, amen.

When I lie down I think, "How long
before I get up?" The night drags on,
and I toss and turn until dawn.

JOB 7:4

*H*ave you ever felt like Job did when
he spoke these words? Has life ever
been so complicated and stressful that you've
tossed and turned, unable to sleep, mulling
over your situation until the birds sang their
morning songs?

Job had reason to toss and turn. Everything
had been stripped away from him—his wealth,
key relationships, his health. In this desperate
state, Job mourned.

Mourning comes before dancing. When
we learn to mourn well, we have greater capacity to live well. At the end of the book of Job,
he shared how, in his former life prior to tragedy, he had only heard God. But now, after
experiencing tragedy, he had seen God.

So take heart. You may have tossed and
turned last night. God may seem far away.
But as you work through your worries, you will
begin to see God in the midst of your circumstances. Morning comes after mourning.

Lord, help me as I grieve. Please remind
me today that the morning is coming,
and your presence is assured, amen.

PEACE-
MAKERS
who sow
in PEACE
reap a
HARVEST
of
righteousness.

JAMES 3:18

Peacemakers who sow in peace reap
a harvest of righteousness.

JAMES 3:18

Sowing and reaping and harvest—these are basic agricultural terms that are helpful in communicating spiritual truth.

For instance, when individuals who love the Lord sow seeds of peace, many benefit from the righteous behavior that results. But just like the role of a farmer, the role of peacemaker can be challenging. After all, we have to fight against our human nature—our sin nature—to choose peace over anger, to make our concern for others more important than our desire to be understood or our angry reactions, and to die to our own wishes and emotions for the sake of the relationship or community.

Being a person of peace helps us as well as those around us live rightly in God's kingdom. Peace, for instance, fosters calmness, rational thinking, and even time for prayer before speaking and acting—all of which improve the odds that we'll make right and righteous choices. Peacemakers help others resolve quarrels and part as friends. Peacemakers gently bring reconciliation to the world.

Lord, use me as a peacemaker in any and
every situation you call me to, amen.

January 16

*A father to the fatherless, a defender of
widows, is God in his holy dwelling.*

PSALM 68:5

Granted, not all of us are fatherless or have experienced widowhood, but we have all walked through heartache on this earth. Each of us has encountered mistreatment or loss or abandonment. We all know what it's like to feel small or overlooked.

The psalmist reminds us of something important about God: he is a personal God. He tailors his interactions with his children based on our needs. To those without a father, he becomes a doting dad. To those who have lost husbands, God takes on the role of protector and defender.

Maybe you desperately need to know today that God loves you in a very personal way. Maybe you need him to be the best friend you lost, or the coach who moved away, or the stepparent who passed on to eternity. Whatever you need, God sits right now in his holy dwelling, ready and able to step in. He is a personal God. He longs to meet your very real needs today, and he is just a prayer away.

*Lord, thank you that you are all that I
need to make it through this day, amen.*

"Do not worry about tomorrow, for tomorrow will worry about itself. Each day has enough trouble of its own."

MATTHEW 6:34

Jesus knew that worrying about tomorrow serves no good purpose. You can't know what the day will bring, and you most likely couldn't change the circumstances if you did. All you can know is today, and that gives us plenty to think about and pray about and deal with and manage. So instead of letting your mind wander to tomorrow, assess your today:

Are you clothed?

Do you have food to eat?

Does God love you?

Is God providing for your needs?

If things today aren't right, ask God to help you change what you can and then pray about those things you can't. Tomorrow will come, and you can do the same thing then. But to worry needlessly about something unknown simply adds more stress to your life. That kind of worry doesn't build your faith muscle, it distracts you from the present, and it interferes with your relationships. Don't let tomorrow steal joy from today.

Lord, help me to see your blessings today. I will let them fuel my trust in you for tomorrow, amen.

"God so loved the world that he gave his one and only Son, that whoever believes in him shall not perish but have eternal life."

JOHN 3:16

Death can be terrifying. Many people spend their lives dreading, fearing, or trying to ignore this inevitability. Yet none of us can escape death.

Thankfully, there is more to the story than our life and inevitable death. After all, there is a dash that will be inserted between the day we're born and the day we die. That dash represents the life we lead on this earth.

Do you truly believe the often-quoted John 3:16? God gave you an amazing gift: his Son, Jesus. And if you spend the dash—that is, the years of your life—believing, trusting in, and following him or if—like the thief on the cross—you put your belief in Jesus in your last moments (see Luke 23:40–43), you will experience eternal life.

Because of Jesus, you can face death only with confidence, and that means you can live this life with peace and joy. What a gift!

Lord, thank you for the precious gifts of love, joy, peace, and eternal life with you, amen.

But as for me, I watch in hope for the LORD.
MICAH 7:7

Watching involves some waiting, and waiting can imply hoping for a certain outcome. To watch in hope for the Lord, then, is to walk through life, with all its struggles, with an expectation that you will see him act.

During this time of waiting and watching, you may experience times of worry. You may feel like God doesn't see your plight or hear your pleas. This is normal. God's plans for you don't always resolve the moment you want them to or the way you might want or expect.

Remember, though, that great stories take time to unfold. The plots of award-winning movies have conflicts and obstacles, and resolution comes only after strife, maybe some confusion, and the passage of time.

Your story is no different. As God writes your story and the plot presents more problems than possible solutions, it's time to exercise your trust muscle. Don't lose hope. Remember that your Father loves you, and believe that he will answer you in his perfect, surprising timing.

Lord, I want to watch for you, to hope for resolution to the plot twists you're bringing about. Grant me patience as I wait, amen.

*Be kind and compassionate to one
another, forgiving each other, just
as in Christ God forgave you.*

EPHESIANS 4:32

*I*magine a mountain, its summit reaching into hazy clouds. Then look along the ground and look for a molehill—a small mound of dirt a mole dredged up.

Now consider this. Your sin against a holy God is taller than the tallest mountain. But the sin committed by one person against you? It's the size of a molehill in comparison. Not that it doesn't matter, or that it didn't hurt (it did!), but in comparison to your mountain of sin against God, that sin against you is small.

That's what Paul was talking about in this verse. Christ has forgiven you a mountain of sin. If you truly believe that fact and are grateful for it, then you can consider your friend or family member's sin against you a small molehill by comparison. Ask God to help you respond to that person with the same compassion and forgiveness you've already received from him. You've been loved and forgiven much. Now you have an opportunity to extend the same love and forgiveness to others.

*Lord, help me to visualize my mountain
of sin when I have an opportunity
to forgive a molehill, amen.*

The Lord is my rock, my fortress and my deliverer.

Psalm 18:2

The LORD is my rock, my fortress and my deliverer; my God is my rock, in whom I take refuge, my shield and the horn of my salvation, my stronghold.

PSALM 18:2

*L*ook at all the words in this single verse that suggest strength: *rock, fortress, deliverer, refuge, shield,* and *stronghold.* Each of these is what God wants to be for you, his child. He is solid. He protects. He sets free. He keeps us safe. He is strong.

Did you notice in this list "the horn of salvation"? Scholars believe the horn is another reference to God's power, and the context definitely supports that idea. This horn is not a musical instrument, but the horn of a bull. This incredibly strong and dangerous animal can gouge a person with one of its horns. The bull's extreme and potentially deadly power is to be feared.

Likewise, we are to fear God. We are to hold him in awe because of his great holiness and infinite power. Thankfully, he uses his strength for our good—to guide us, to love us, and to help us live our lives in his strength alone.

Lord, thank you for using your power on my behalf, amen.

January 22

*I command you to be openhanded
toward your fellow Israelites who are
poor and needy in your land.*

DEUTERONOMY 15:11

It's easy to become desensitized to the needs of the poor, particularly if we live in suburban America. We forget the struggles our nation's working poor face every single day, and on TV we're confronted by worldwide poverty.

Jesus taught that we'll always have the poor with us. Yet when we look at Jesus' life on this earth, we will see just how much he valued the poor. He stopped to talk with them. He healed them. He even said the poor were blessed. Why? Because poor people know their great need for God.

Now, if we say we love God, then we will value what and whom he valued.

So look around you. Maybe a friend is struggling to pay a bill, or a child in the Philippines needs sponsorship, or a young woman in your community needs a Big Sister. Prayerfully ask Jesus to show you where he wants you to help meet the needs of the poor.

*Lord, I want to be openhanded when it
comes to people in need. Enable me to
give generously and joyfully, amen.*

Mary has chosen what is BETTER and it will not be TAKEN AWAY from her.

LUKE 10:42

"Martha, Martha . . . you are worried and upset about many things. . . . Mary has chosen what is better, and it will not be taken away from her."

LUKE 10:42

Martha and Mary often welcomed Jesus into their home. Gracious hostesses, they willingly fed Jesus and his disciples. Loving her ministry of hospitality and the opportunity to serve others, Martha spent much time preparing.

Mary served Jesus, too, but in an entirely different way. Hers was not the tangible service of preparing a meal. She did not chop vegetables or bake bread. No, she sat quietly at his feet, listening to him teach. In that quiet place at his sacred feet, she honored him and worshipped him. She gave him the precious gift of her undivided attention.

Although Martha's service was necessary and appreciated, she chose activity in the kitchen over adoration at Jesus' feet. She didn't realize that this Someone was more important than meeting the physical needs of her guests. That's why Jesus praised Mary's actions over Martha's. Here, devotion was a wiser choice than service.

Lord, I want my life to be more about devotion than service today and every day. Oh, how I love you! Amen.

"In the same way, let your light shine before others, that they may see your good deeds and glorify your Father in heaven."

MATTHEW 5:16

We read verses like this and nod, *Oh, yes! I want to shine so others see Jesus in me.* But what does that really mean?

To understand Jesus' instructions, we have to back up to the previous verse where Jesus said, "Neither do people light a lamp and put it under a bowl. Instead they put it on its stand, and it gives light to everyone in the house" (v. 15). In order for the lamp to provide good light, it must be placed where others can benefit from it.

Being a light isn't about trying hard to be one. It is about being gloriously you in the midst of your life, loving Jesus and pointing to Him. To think *Well, I'm not special. What do I have to offer?* is to forcibly remove yourself from the lampstand God has given you.

Wherever you are today, dare to shine. Embrace the place God has for you.

Lord, I'm glad that I don't have to try to be a light. Use me to shine brightly where you have me, amen.

*The LORD is my light and my
salvation—whom shall I fear?*

PSALM 27:1

*M*any of us spend time worrying what others think about us and even re-orienting our lives in order to make others happy with us. The problem is, living to please others can be exhausting. Furthermore, we really can't control what other people think about us anyway.

The truth is, what others think of you doesn't matter as much as what God thinks of you. God is on your side, and he is your Defender. As this psalm says, God is your light—even if you feel shrouded in darkness. He is your salvation—it's not up to you to save yourself. And he is your Stronghold—a very real fortress.

Because of these important truths, you no longer need to live in fear of other people's opinions. You can instead walk through life in holy confidence that God is always with you despite what others say and no matter how your reputation has been tarnished. God will always hold you, protect you, and shield you.

*Lord, instead of worrying about what
others think, help me to realize that
if I have your love—and I do—I have
all I need in this life, amen.*

If we are thrown into the blazing furnace, the God we serve is able to deliver us from it, and he will deliver us from Your Majesty's hand.

DANIEL 3:17

The most powerful statement in this story of Shadrach, Meshach, and Abednego comes in the next verse. Here, in verse 17, they assert God's power, but in verse 18, they praise and affirm God's sovereignty as well as submit to it. They say—paraphrased—"But even if God doesn't save us, we want to make it clear to you, Your Majesty, that we will never serve your gods or worship the gold statue you have set up."

"But even if he doesn't."

Yes, God can deliver you. But you cannot know the entirety of his plan. Sometimes your story will involve pain. When that's the case, you can still confidently say, "My God is strong. He is able to deliver me," and then, in the next breath, declare your loyalty: "But even if he doesn't."

Maybe you're facing something like that right now. Rest in knowing God has a plan even if circumstances are fiery.

Lord, I want to declare, "But even if you don't!" Give me the faith to trust your sovereign rule, amen.

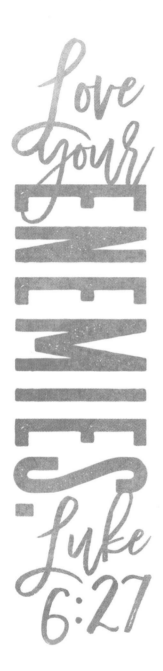

*"Love your enemies, do good to those
who hate you, bless those who curse you,
pray for those who mistreat you."*

LUKE 6:27-28

Here, Jesus instructed his disciples about how to live as he did on the earth. Specifically, Jesus didn't ask them—and he doesn't ask us who are his disciples today—to do anything he himself hadn't already done.

Jesus did good to those who hated him: he willingly gave up his life on a cross so that every enemy of God—and that is the entire human race—could be forgiven for their sins and have eternal life.

Jesus blessed those who cursed him: from the cross, he asked God to forgive those in charge of the crucifixion because they didn't know what they were doing.

Jesus prayed with compassion and understanding for those who mistreated and mistreat him today (see John 17).

Because he set this example—and because his Spirit lives within you—you can do the impossible. And when you do, you'll be set free from bitterness.

*Lord, I can love those who hate me
only in your strength and with your
help, so please help me, amen.*

Faith comes from hearing the message, and the message is heard through the word about Christ.

ROMANS 10:17

What is God like? A lot of big words can describe him: omniscient, omnipotent, omnipresent, immutable, and sovereign, for instance. Each of those is absolutely true—and pretty hard to completely get our minds around.

There's another way we can know what God is like, and that's by getting to know Jesus. In the written Word—the Bible—we can read about what God is like, but in the living Word—in Jesus—we can see what God really is like. The essence of God is love, and Jesus is the exact representation of love in human form.

Think about the love you see in how Jesus lived. Healing the blind. Raising the dead. Feeding the hungry. Touching the leper. Forgiving the prostitute. Respecting women. Praying for his disciples. And, yes, dying on the cross. These actions speak loudly of God's love, and his acts of love continue today. Sit quietly and listen for him to speak. When he does, he speaks love over you.

Lord, I want to walk in your love, share your love with others, and love you with all that I am, amen.

Man does not live on bread alone.
DEUTERONOMY 8:3

Man does not live on bread alone but on every
word that comes from the mouth of the LORD.

DEUTERONOMY 8:3

When Jesus was being tempted by Satan in the wilderness, Jesus said these words when the enemy suggested he turn the stones into bread. Imagine not eating for forty days! This mention of making your own loaves of bread out of rocks would be entirely tempting.

Although he was hungry, Jesus found truth in God's Word that helped him stand strong against the evil one. Jesus quoted Moses, who, in Deuteronomy, was instructing the nation of Israel how to live in in a way that would honor and please the Lord. Remember, God had brought the people of Israel through the Red Sea on dry land. He had sustained them in the wilderness with water and manna. Moses wanted the people to keep their eyes and hearts set on the Provider, not on the provisions.

More intensely than your physical hunger screams to be satisfied, your heart longs to be filled by God. Only he can nurture you and sustain you in this journey called life.

Lord, I want to feast on your words
today and always, amen.

*"You will receive power when the Holy
Spirit comes on you; and you will be my
witnesses in Jerusalem, and in all Judea and
Samaria, and to the ends of the earth."*

ACTS 1:8

*T*he word *witness* here in the Greek is *mar-
tus,* from which we get the word *martyr.*
What's powerful about this etymology is that
when the Holy Spirit comes upon you, God
gives you the ability to be a martyr for his sake.

In our everyday world, we are—by God's
grace—far removed from martyrdom. In fact,
many of us can't even fathom being killed for
our faith in Jesus, yet fellow believers are dying
at an alarming rate around the world. If you've
ever thought, *I could never die for my faith,* realize that God will enable you to do anything he
calls you to do. After all, his infinite power now
dwells within you.

You may not face physical death for your
faith, but you may face great opposition. Know
that the Holy Spirit will enable you to stand up
for what you believe, to be kind when you'd
rather shout back, and to love your enemies.

*Lord, thank you for empowering me
to be strong in you today, amen.*

*"Though your sins are like scarlet,
they shall be as white as snow."*

ISAIAH 1:18

This image comes in Isaiah's prophecy of a time when the sins of the human race would yet be atoned for by One who was sinless, pure, and unmarred by corruption. The prophet aptly described our sins as scarlet, the color of fresh blood, of the spilled blood of Jesus that meant forgiveness of our sins and a cleansing that would leave us "white as snow."

Jesus bled and died for our sakes, so we could enter into a relationship with God. Jesus was the perfect sacrifice for our sins. Because of this amazing act of love and grace, we no longer need to try to earn our way into God's presence or prove our worth in his sight. God has already declared us clean and welcomed us as his children. What beauty comes from knowing that the holy God sees us as worth loving! And he sees us that way because, acting in love, Jesus gave himself as a sacrifice, once and for all, for our sins.

Hallelujah! What a Savior!

*Lord Jesus, thank you for dying for my
sins, that I may be cleansed of them. I
am humbled and grateful, amen.*

February

He says, "Be still, and know that I am God; I will be exalted among the nations, I will be exalted in the earth."

PSALM 46:10

We are rushers. We run here and there, too rarely enjoying each sacred moment. One reason we run is our lack of trust. We don't necessarily believe God knows what he is doing, so we pick up the slack and live as if everything depended upon us.

This psalm reminds us that all that hurried rushing ends in . . . nothing. Whether you run yourself ragged or sit quietly in a chair, God will ultimately be exalted all over the earth. His purposes will always prevail.

The psalmist must have known that we are inclined to hurry, and he gives us the key to slowing down: know God. When we seek to know God and his ways, we suddenly realize that he is God, and we are not.

God loves you whether you tend to run or relax. Take a moment right now to stop, to listen, to be present in the moment.

Lord, I am grateful you carry out your purposes all around the world. Help me to rest in your sovereign goodness today, amen.

*"I will give you a new heart and put a new
spirit in you; I will remove from you your
heart of stone and give you a heart of flesh."*

EZEKIEL 36:26

What do you see as the most interesting word in this verse? I think the word *I* is, hands down, the most interesting. I find it fascinating that God is the One—the "I"— who will give us a brand-new heart and infuse a brand-new spirit. He takes away our stony hearts and gives us a heart that feels, prays, sympathizes, worships, and so much more.

Now consider the fact that it is God who does all the good work in your life. He orchestrated your renewal by sending his Son to die for you on the cross. And, because of him, your heart is made brand-new, alive, and fresh.

Guard and protect the heart that God has given you. Be quick to forgive. Run from bitterness. Work toward reconciliation. Love lavishly. This is your daily response to a God who made your heart and your spirit brand-new.

*Lord, I thank you for giving me a new
heart. Please help me protect it—and as
I do so, may you be glorified, amen.*

MY BROTHERS & SISTERS, REJOICE IN THE LORD! PHILIPPIANS 3:1

Rejoice in the Lord!

PHILIPPIANS 3:1

Throughout his letter to the Philippian believers, the apostle Paul wrote about joy and rejoicing. That theme reflects his passion for them—that they would begin to live out the joy that Jesus demonstrated when he walked this earth.

Rejoicing doesn't come naturally to us. We tend to see the world through the lens of pessimism, and if too many hard and sad things happen at once, they darken our mood and silence our joy.

But Paul reminded us that joy is a choice. No matter where you find yourself today—in the midst of a too-busy life, navigating difficult relationships, worried about finances, burdened by children's decisions—you can choose joy. Sound impossible? Ask Jesus to help you. He would love to reorient your perspective and give you a heart of gratitude.

So today instead of recounting your worries, choose joy by counting the many blessings God has brought your way. He loves to open your eyes to hope in him, and he will help you see the goodness all around you.

*Lord, I choose joy today, and I am
going to start by counting at least
ten blessings right now, amen.*

*If any of you lacks wisdom, you should ask
God, who gives generously to all without
finding fault, and it will be given to you.*

JAMES 1:5

Our generous God loves to give us wisdom. That's why James reminded us that when we're bewildered by life, we can ask God directly for wisdom.

And God is not an angry PE teacher who slaps you upside the head if you can't do a pull-up. The Scripture assures that God is happy to give wisdom "without finding fault."

You may be facing a bewildering situation and can't figure out what to do. Or perhaps you have no idea how to answer that person who is aggressively questioning your beliefs. Or maybe you have no idea how to parent a now-wayward child. The good news: you don't have to figure out any of this—you don't have to figure out anything—on your own. God loves you, and he wants to generously provide you with wisdom. Just ask.

*Lord, I need wisdom today. Thank
you in advance. I'm grateful you
are a generous God, amen.*

Do not turn from it to the right or to the left.

JOSHUA
1:7

"Do not turn from it to the right or to the left,
that you may be successful wherever you go."

JOSHUA 1:7

We live in a distracted world. Its shiny things attract us while we're serving the Lord, raising kids, or working to pay bills. The world's noise makes it tough for us to hear God's voice. Yet these two activities—listening to God and being focused on him—are critical for Christ followers.

To hear God we must pull away from this crazy world and be quiet. The beautiful thing about this need to pull away is that it doesn't take much time or effort. You can, for example, drive in a silent car where you can listen for the Lord to speak to you.

Once we've been encouraged and directed by God's voice, we can then choose to focus on exactly what he would have us focus on. He is pleased when we choose to do the specific things he asks us to do rather than wavering or flitting from here to there.

Lord, I want to hear your voice with clarity
and then obey it with energy and joy, amen.

*After Job had prayed for his friends, the
Lord restored his fortunes and gave him
twice as much as he had before.*

JOB 42:10

Without knowing the context of this verse, you might think the simple act of praying for others results in great wealth. That's not the takeaway here!

First, a little background. Remember that Job's friends didn't act like friends. Although they began well (they sat with him, grieving quietly, saying nothing), they didn't continue well. The moment they each opened their mouths, words of discouragement flowed.

So Job praying for his friends is a more difficult act than merely throwing a prayer heavenward. When he prayed for them, a whole lot of pain, unforgiveness, and bitterness existed between them. In order to pray, Job had to deal with his own lack of forgiveness.

There is something powerful about choosing to let go of pain, of sharing it openly with God, of choosing to forgive those who wronged you. When you do this, you'll experience a soul richness and inexplicable peace. You'll be set free from bitterness. That is wealth, indeed.

*Lord, I want the soul richness you
offer. I choose to forgive my friend
today. Please help me, amen.*

*I praise you because I am fearfully
and wonderfully made; your works are
wonderful, I know that full well.*

PSALM 139:14

It's easy to look at someone else and see how fearfully, wonderfully, and beautifully God made her! We know "full well" that he did excellent work when he made . . . *other people.*

But when you look in the mirror, do you believe you are "fearfully and wonderfully made," lovingly crafted by your Creator? Do you believe he delights in you and thinks you are wonderful? Believing that you are beautifully crafted by your loving God is very difficult. After all, our culture pushes hard against this thought.

Thanks to our culture's various media, we easily see our flaws. We notice wrinkles before anyone else does. We can't seem to help comparing ourselves to people in our lives and photos on grocery-store magazine covers.

The truth is, you are beautiful. God created you. He loves you. He cherishes you. And he is saddened when you are down on yourself or criticize your looks. But you can bring him great joy when you accept your great worth in his sight.

*Lord, please help me know "full well"
that I am beautiful, amen.*

"I will give them an undivided heart and put a new spirit in them; I will remove from them their heart of stone and give them a heart of flesh."

EZEKIEL 11:19

An undivided heart is rare these days. All of us are pulled in a hundred different directions. No wonder each of us walks this earth scattered—mentally, emotionally, and spiritually.

So what does it mean to have an undivided heart when it comes to our relationship with God? It means we make him the most important Person, thought, and focus in our lives. We let him take precedence over everything and everyone. Sounds simple and straightforward, right? But the behavior is definitely not intuitive for us.

This verse from Ezekiel teaches that an undivided heart and a new spirit are both gifts from God. We are able to receive them after God removes our hard hearts and gives us new life.

So be encouraged! You may feel pulled in various directions, but God is at work in you, giving you an undivided heart. Rest in that. Be at peace.

Lord, I'm thankful you have given me an undivided heart in this very divided world, amen.

Whether you turn to the right or to the left, your ears will hear a voice behind you, saying, "This is the way; walk in it."

ISAIAH 30:21

$\mathcal{L}$ ife can be confusing, particularly when you're trying to make important decisions about your future and need guidance from the Lord.

Isaiah the prophet was in such a situation: he was trying to hear God's instructions for an entire nation! So this promise from God was especially encouraging.

But what can you do when you don't hear God's voice, when his direction isn't clear and doesn't seem forthcoming? First, remember that God speaks in a variety of ways.

Go to God's Word. When you need wisdom, spend some time reading in the book of Proverbs and meditating on those truths.

Go to God's body. When you're confused about your next step, ask a Christian friend for advice. Share your story openly, ask for counsel, and pray together for discernment.

Go to God himself. Pray directly to him, asking him for help.

Lord, I need to know what my next step is. Please give me wisdom through your Word, through your people, or now as I listen, amen.

*Always give yourselves fully to the work
of the Lord, because you know that
your labor in the Lord is not in vain.*

1 CORINTHIANS 15:58

*P*lunging ourselves headlong into the work of God can result in burnout. We can work so hard, pray so hard, serve so hard, and then, in the end, burn out so hard. That's not what Paul was exhorting us to do!

The "work of the Lord" is to love, and love is manifest in countless ways. But there are many ways that no one except the Lord himself sees. Perhaps you anonymously gave money to a friend in need. Or you prayed for a suffering neighbor who had no idea you were doing so. Or you wrote letters to inmates. God sees all of this.

Such work is not in vain. As you reach out with God's love, he may use you to bring that person to a saving knowledge of him. With God's blessing, your work will have eternal results.

*Lord, I'm weary. Please help me remember
that the work I do for you and for
others in your name is not in vain but
will have eternal results, amen.*

"ALL AUTHORITY

IN HEAVEN AND ON EARTH HAS BEEN GIVEN TO ME."

MATTHEW 28:18

*Jesus came to [the eleven disciples]
and said, "All authority in heaven and
on earth has been given to me."*

MATTHEW 28:18

When asked what the first word of the Great Commission is, most people answer "Go"—as in "Go and make disciples of all nations" (v. 19). But the first word isn't *go*; the first word is *all*. As Jesus commissioned us to share his love with a dying world, his first word was the all-encompassing word *all*.

And all authority in the world as well as in heaven was his. He is Creator of everything and therefore the genuine Authority over every single institution and government.

We gain a sweet perspective on our lives and even on the state of the world when we think about Jesus' supremacy. No matter what you're facing today, he has all the authority over the situations you're concerned about. Jesus is King. He is Ruler over all. Rest in him and trust him to see you through *all* your problems.

Lord, thank you that you have all authority in heaven and on earth. So I will choose to entrust to you my stressful situation today, amen.

He was pierced for our transgressions,
he was crushed for our iniquities; the
punishment that brought us peace was on
him, and by his wounds we are healed.

ISAIAH 53:5

*A*lthough Isaiah prophesied these verses hundreds of years before Jesus was born, they proved stunningly true. Jesus was speared ("pierced") in his side during his crucifixion. He was flogged and beaten raw for the sake of our sin ("iniquities"). As Jesus hung on the cross ("wounds"), God poured out on his own Son his wrath against sin: the perfect Lamb was sacrificed, and divine justice was satisfied, providing for us the opportunity to have a relationship with our holy God ("healed").

A beautiful thing about Jesus is that he truly understands what it means to walk this earth. He understands being wounded by the world. He is well acquainted with betrayal, rejection, lies, loneliness, and people's anger and hatred. He understands what you experience. You can tell your Savior anything. And he will listen and understand.

Lord Jesus, thank you for dying on the cross for
me so that my sins are forgiven. And thank you
for living on this earth for another reason too: I
know you understand what I go through! Amen.

*From that time on Jesus began to
preach, "Repent, for the kingdom
of heaven has come near."*

MATTHEW 4:17

To repent is to change the direction you're headed. It's to stop walking on the road you're traveling and instead go another way. It's to acknowledge that your way of living isn't working and choosing a better option. In the context of the kingdom of God, repenting means acknowledging your sin before a holy God, asking for forgiveness, and—relying on his strength—no longer being involved in that behavior.

But repenting doesn't happen once and for all. Genuine repentance means continuing to walk according to God's ways. It's to live according to his two most important commands: love God with all you are and love your neighbor as yourself. Instead of walking the popular route of the world, we follow in the footsteps of Jesus, asking his Spirit to help us to live like Jesus.

Are you living a lifestyle of repentance, of turning from your sinful desires and living to please and glorify God?

*Lord, by your Spirit, may my thoughts,
attitudes, and actions please you, amen.*

The fruit of the righteous is a tree of life,
and the one who is wise saves lives.

PROVERBS 11:30

Why is it important to chase after wisdom? It's necessary for our own sake. Reading through the book of Proverbs—a chapter a day—will help you make wise decisions, the kinds of decisions that bring soul health and soul prosperity.

But there's another aspect to wisdom you may not realize. According to this verse, wisdom saves lives. Wisdom is important not merely for your sake: wisdom allows you to walk alongside others, helping them navigate their lives. You might, for instance, be able to warn people who are about to do self-destructive things. You can help a friend steer clear of financial disaster. Acts like these are ways of saving lives on this earth.

God is gracious to you in so many ways, but he does not gift you with righteousness and wisdom only for your sake. He blesses you so you can bless others. He grants you wisdom for your own life journey and so that you can help others avoid bad decisions. What a privilege!

Lord, I need your wisdom today, not only for myself, but for the sake of those I love, amen.

May God be gracious to us and bless
us and make his face shine on us.

PSALM 67:1

*L*ook around the auditorium when the junior high band has a concert. What do you see? Parents and relatives of the band members. One couple's faces shine with joy over their child's clarinet solo. And that image reflects God's face shining upon us.

God, our heavenly Father, watches our lives like a proud parent, reveling in our efforts, filled with joy as he looks at us. But we don't have to perform to make him smile. He flat out loves us in the midst of our messiness too.

Today's Scripture reminds us that God's desires to be gracious to us and to bless us. And his gracious blessing comes often in the form of his affection and kindness toward us.

You may have had a difficult parent whose face didn't shine on you. Or maybe you feel God is mad at you, and his face couldn't possibly light up when he sees you. The truth is this: God's face shines with joy when he thinks of you.

*Lord, I'm humbled by imagining your face
actually shining when you think of me—
and I'm grateful for your love, amen.*

"Then the master told his servant, 'Go out to the roads and country lanes and compel them to come in, so that my house will be full.'"

LUKE 14:23

I think it's a misnomer: we call it social media, but it's a means of interacting that is anything but social.

Instead of hiding behind screens, we need to be interacting with real people face-to-face. And that can mean putting our phones down and going to actually be with a person. Yes, it is a countercultural yet loving act to go to people wherever they are. But that act reveals just how much people matter to God—and to you.

May it be that no matter where you find yourself today, you are living in light of Jesus' command to love people where they live. This can simply be a kind interaction at the grocery store, or saying a short prayer for a friend who is struggling, or making a meal for a friend. You are obeying the second greatest commandment by loving others well.

Lord, guide me to those people who need a touch of your love, and use me, I pray, to provide that, amen.

THE PATH OF THE RIGHTEOUS IS LIKE THE MORNING SUN. Proverbs 4:18

The path of the righteous is like the morning sun, shining ever brighter till the full light of day.

PROVERBS 4:18

When Peter stood in the boat while Jesus beckoned him to step out onto the wave-chopped water, he could not know whether the water would hold him up. Still, he took one faithful step, then another. Peter chose to trust Jesus' ability to sustain him in the storm, and Jesus came through (see Matthew 14:22–33).

Life works like that for us as well. Maybe Jesus has been beckoning you toward something new. You cannot see around the bend in the road, but you can experience peace and joy when you take that Peter-like first step. Today's verse reminds us that as we keep walking on the path of faith, the light by which God guides can become brighter, and we may gain greater understanding.

So be assured that even if the path Jesus takes you on gets scary, he will always be there to illuminate your way—and rescue you if necessary.

Lord, thank you that you are with me when you ask me to take a step of faith. Please help me to have the faith to step into new adventures with you, amen.

February 18

"My Father's house has many rooms; if that were not so, would I have told you that I am going there to prepare a place for you?"

JOHN 14:2

We are vagabonds on this earth, roaming, moving, looking for a place to call home. An entire industry (HGTV, anyone?) has flourished because of this very real desire. Whether you've moved around or stayed put, the truth remains: we long to feel at home.

So to hear that Jesus fully understands this longing is great news. He knows that we were made for a specific person and a specific place. As author Randy Alcorn says, God is that Person, and heaven is that place. As you sojourn on this earth, Jesus is fashioning the perfect place for you—one that fits every desire and need for beauty.

When we get close to death, one of the things we wrestle with is leaving our families, friends, and the places that are familiar to us. Yet the book of Revelation describes people, rivers, cities, meals, mountains—things we know on earth that will be Technicolor in heaven.

Lord, thank you that you're creating a perfect place for me—and that this perfect place is with you, amen.

The Lord is not slow in keeping his promise

2 PETER 3:9

The Lord is not slow in keeping his promise,
as some understand slowness. Instead he
is patient with you, not wanting anyone to
perish, but everyone to come to repentance.

2 PETER 3:9

A good way to see the Lord's patience with us is to look back on our lives and see when and how he worked. At times we strayed from him. Sometimes we were indifferent to him. Even so, he pursued us.

Jesus wants us to be patient like he was when we consider the journeys of those we love. We must be patient when our loved ones are straying or indifferent. We can pray that God brings them to the point of repentance.

If you're discouraged about a loved one's journey, remember two things. First, you cannot make a person repent. That is one of the Holy Spirit's jobs. Second—as today's verse says—God is not slow in keeping his promise to your loved ones. He is wooing them. He is patient. Trust that he loves your loved ones far more than you do.

Lord, I surrender my loved ones to you.
I trust you to be patient with them as
you invite them to repentance, amen.

*"Suppose one of you has a hundred sheep
and loses one of them. Doesn't he leave
the ninety-nine in the open country and
go after the lost sheep until he finds it?"*

LUKE 15:4

This verse offers great encouragement to those who love prodigals—friends or family members who have wandered off into places that seem far away from God and unreachable.

The truth is, God loves your prodigal far more than you do. This truth is hard to grasp, particularly if the prodigal is your child. But Jesus' love for his children is relentless: he tirelessly seeks after those who run away, who are lost, who are wayward.

Perhaps it will help to envision the scene in this verse as you pray for a prodigal. Imagine Jesus leaving the sheepfold, walking through the gate and beyond green mountains in search of that sheep. He continues his search until he finds the lamb he loves.

Do you realize that Jesus did this for you? Jesus sought you. He looked for you in distant fields, but he didn't hesitate. Jesus' love is the kind that pursues and seeks. Rest in that knowledge today.

*Lord, I'm grateful that you relentlessly pursue
lost people. Please find my prodigal, amen.*

I PRESS ON TOWARD THE GOAL.

PHILIPPIANS 3:14

I press on toward the goal to win the prize for which God has called me heavenward in Christ Jesus.

PHILIPPIANS 3:14

If you've ever run in a race, you know those moments when you feel like giving up. Sometimes the only thing that keeps you huffing and puffing along is the prize awaiting you at the finish line. And sometimes the prize is simply crossing that line.

It's the same in our lives. Obstacles prevent us from moving forward, so with God's power we jump over them. Our strength falls away, so we ask God for his supernatural strength to face the next trial. Grief makes us breathless, so we mourn, Jesus alongside, and we determine to keep walking.

Why do we keep going? Why do we persevere?

Because the race has a finish line. Someday, God will reward us for finishing the race he mapped out for us. He will have noticed our quiet victories on earth. He knows and understands every moment of our race.

So keep moving. Keep taking one step after another. Reaching the finish line will be worth it.

Lord, I'm weary of this race. Please help me— empower me—to press on to the end, amen.

"When you stand praying, if you hold anything against anyone, forgive them, so that your Father in heaven may forgive you your sins."

MARK 11:25

Our sins against a holy, beautiful God are many, yet he has chosen to forgive us, to pardon us for our waywardness and willfulness. The right response to that outrageous generosity is to learn from it, and then give it away to others. Your choice to forgive reflects the depth of your gratitude to God for his forgiveness of your sin. The more grateful you are for his forgiveness, the more freely you will forgive those who have hurt you.

Forgiveness isn't easy, and it isn't to be offered lightly. After all, forgiveness is a radical choice that acknowledges the pain, grieves the sin, and then turns the situation on its head by forgiving the guilty one. Forgiveness frees you to love anew the people in your life. It opens your heart and releases you from bitterness. It gives you joy as your heart escapes from the prison of wanting to enact punishment or seek revenge.

Lord, I choose to forgive that person who hurt me. Thank you for forgiving me, amen.

*If a ruler listens to lies, all his
officials become wicked.*

PROVERBS 29:12

Deception is like cancer: it invades and destroys those near it. This is why truth is so vitally important. When we tell the truth about ourselves, we are set free to be ourselves. When we see the world through the lens of God's truth, we discern good choices and are better equipped to fight on behalf of justice. But if we actively listen to lies, not only can we forget truth, but we also run the risk of affecting—infecting—those we love.

It's hard not to hear lies today. Just turn on your computer, the TV, your handheld device. You'll hear that you have to look a certain way to have worth; you have to have specific things to be valuable in this world. Lies swirl around us in a toxic soup, and we can have a hard time discerning the truth.

None of the world's lies reflects Jesus Christ, his love, his values, his priorities, or his truth about your value. Make time each day to review the truths of who you are in Jesus.

*Lord, today, I choose truth. I choose
to believe you've made me beautiful
and you love me, amen.*

Jesus replied: "Love the Lord your God
with all your heart and with all your
soul and with all your mind."

MATTHEW 22:37

Jesus longs for us to love him with everything we are—our heart, soul, and mind. What does that mean in practical terms? The easiest way to explain this kind of all-encompassing love is to look at the life of Brother Lawrence. He served in a Carmelite monastery in the 1600s, and he is best known for "practicing the presence of God."

This meant that all throughout the day, he maintained a continual conversation with God. He thanked God that he had the ability to do dishes for his glory. He interacted with God while he swept. He tried to view the world through God-colored glasses.

So, loving God with all your heart, soul, and mind is as simple as cultivating a continual conversation with Jesus all day long. Despite life's responsibilities and distractions, you can still choose to connect with Jesus right now. He will welcome you as you practice being aware of his presence with you!

Lord, I do want to love you with everything
within me. Teach me how to have a continual
conversation with you today, amen.

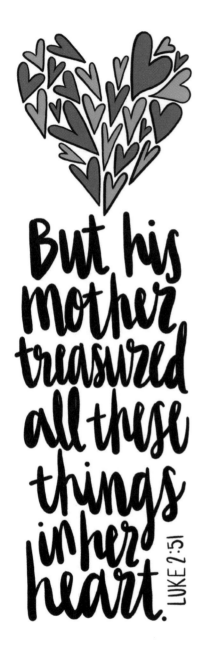

*But his mother treasured all
these things in her heart.*

LUKE 2:51

Imagine if Mary, the mother of Jesus, had had Instagram! She could have shared pictures of the Son of Man every single moment of his anointed life, starting at the manger. Instead, though, Mary did something quite the opposite. Instead of sharing with the world everything on her mind, she instead thought deeply about every moment, undoubtedly hoping to sear each into her heart and mind.

That's what treasure is for, not for trumpeting but for cherishing. Imagine all the wonders Mary experienced. She could've built quite a Twitter presence, but even if she'd had the technology, I think she would have held back. She shared intimate secrets only with her God. Perhaps aware that sharing them would cheapen them, Mary chose to treasure every experience.

We would do well to follow her countercultural example. Instead of rushing to post our every experience and thought, we might find it more satisfying to pull away from technology, draw near to God, and spend some time with him.

*Lord, I choose today to treasure
evidence of your goodness to me rather
than instantly report it, amen.*

"I looked for someone among them who would build up the wall and stand before me in the gap on behalf of the land so I would not have to destroy it, but I found no one."

EZEKIEL 22:30

*J*n this verse, God was speaking to the nation of Israel. The longing in his father-heart is evident: he wants to spare his people from destruction. Unfortunately no one was willing to stand in the gap and pray for the nation.

Jesus was the ultimate answer to God's aching heart of love. Jesus stood in the gap between God's holiness and our depravity.

And on the cross Jesus boldly bridged that gap, dying in your place and welcoming you to a relationship with God.

This eternal plan of divine and immeasurable grace is almost too much to fathom—this God who answers his own pleas for his people. He became the means for rescue. For your rescue.

Rest on that truth today: Jesus stands in the gap for you. The cross was the bridge, and he loves you enough to bear the nails.

Lord Jesus, thank you for standing in the gap for me with your very life. I needed to remember that today, amen.

You provide a broad path for my feet,
so that my ankles do not give way.

2 SAMUEL 22:37

*A*t certain times in our lives we simply cannot keep walking. In those times, we desperately need to experience the rest that God has for us. We need to, for instance, experience the lovingkindness he shows by broadening a path and protecting our ankles—two things necessary for walking well and walking long.

Are you worn out? Wearied by the rat race? Stressed beyond measure?

Then perhaps it's time to slow down and ask God to both broaden your path and provide for you a time of rest. Make some time this week to be quiet and still. Then, when you have settled your mind and heart, ask God to adjust your perspective on your circumstances, to speak life where death reigns, and to encourage your weary soul.

God loves you. He wants to help you throughout your journey. And he never wearies of your prayers.

Lord, I desperately need a broad path and a day
or two of deep, deep rest in you. I thank you in
advance for taking care of me yet again, amen.

Do not be misled: "Bad company
corrupts good character."

1 CORINTHIANS 15:33

*I*f you have teens, you've probably shared this truth with them, imploring them to choose their friends wisely. You've seen and perhaps experienced the reality that the people we choose to hang around with can deeply influence the decisions we make and the way we live.

It's easy to think this verse applies to our teens, not us. But consider that today you can interact with all sorts of people and entertain ideas from all around the globe. While that connection can be an awesome blessing, this "company" can also corrupt you.

So who are you keeping company with via the media? What are you spending your time viewing? What influence are those choices having on you? The more we saturate ourselves with bad company, the more corrupt our character can become. So choose your social media and entertainment wisely. Watch things that bring you closer to Jesus, not push you farther away. .

Lord, I surrender to you my viewing habits—
and I know I'll need to every day. Help me
choose to watch only what honors you, amen.

May the God of hope fill you with all
joy and peace as you trust in him,
so that you may overflow with hope
by the power of the Holy Spirit.

ROMANS 15:13

*T*his verse highlights an important but difficult-to-live-out verb: *trust.* Joy and peace come as you exercise your trust muscle. Then hope floods your heart.

Often we ask God for an easier life so we can be happy. Instead, he allows circumstances in our lives that require us to trust him.

And what exactly is trust in God? It's choosing to believe that God sees us, is for us, and will carry us through every situation. Trust is not flashy. Instead, it's a quiet choice we make, knowing that God commands the universe with power and skill—and that includes our universes, where our cares and worries dwell.

No matter where you are today, choose to trust in the ability of God to restore joy, peace, and hope to your heart.

Lord, I confess that it's really hard for
me to trust you. Enable me to see your
faithfulness to me today as I lay down at
your feet my cares and worries, amen.

March

*Many waters cannot quench love;
rivers cannot sweep it away.*

SONG OF SONGS 8:7

March 1

*Many waters cannot quench love;
rivers cannot sweep it away.*

SONG OF SONGS 8:7

God's love is an immovable force, a bountiful feast that never runs out. His love is fixed and assured. Why? Because God is not only the Originator of love, but he *is* love. Love is his very nature. When we read about love in 1 Corinthians 13, we remember that God's love encompasses all those traits: patience, kindness, hope, endurance, and more.

You cannot outrun his love. Nor can you hide from it. His love for you is constant and ever present. He relentlessly pursues you, your heart, your dreams. But he also gives you freedom. Why? Because he loves you.

So what happens if you do run the other way? And what happens when you try to hide? He loves you so much that he won't violate your will. He will allow your wanderings.

The good news is this: right now you can turn toward his radical love. Let go of your rebellion, and then ask him to show you the kind of love that waters can't quench or rivers sweep away.

*Lord, I need that kind of love in my life—
the kind that doesn't ever end, amen.*

Do not be anxious about anything, but in every situation, by prayer and petition, with thanksgiving, present your requests to God.

PHILIPPIANS 4:6

This verse may be very familiar to you, and it's easy to miss the significance of this command. For instance, what exactly does *petition* mean? According to Dictionary.com, a petition is "a request made for something desired, especially a respectful or humble request, as to a superior or to one of those in authority."

At the end of Matthew's gospel, Jesus reassured us that all authority in heaven and on earth had been given to him (see Matthew 28:18). That means when we make our requests, we are asking them of the Supreme Ruler of the universe.

Jesus alone can remedy your stress. So make your anxieties known to the One who, with his unlimited authority, will respond with wisdom and love.

Lord, you are truly Lord of everything. I'm grateful I can share my worries with you, amen.

*Offer your bodies as living sacrifices,
holy and pleasing to God—this is
your spiritual act of worship.*

ROMANS 12:1

*P*aul's words here are wildly counter-cultural. This call to give everything to God, including our bodies, is radical and right. After all, Jesus has done great things on our behalf: at the cross he saved us from the consequences of our sin, from eternal separation from God, the ultimate death. And he did this by giving over his physical body.

In response, we are to do the same. We yield our bodies for his purposes and in his honor, for him to use us in the world according to his perfect plan. Every day we have the opportunity to worship Jesus by dying to our own wishes and plans, by offering ourselves—our bodies—as a living sacrifice for his service. And he calls our doing so a "spiritual act of worship."

Worship is far more than singing songs. Worship is also offering your life—daily, hourly, minute by minute. Surrendering your heart, body, and life means more to God than songs well sung.

*Lord, I offer myself to you for
your good purposes, amen.*

*There is no wisdom, no insight, no plan
that can succeed against the LORD.*

PROVERBS 21:30

We are planners. We want to orchestrate the life we've always desired. Sometimes that manifests itself as an insatiable need for control.

No matter how much you strive to make everything right (from your perspective), God is the sovereign God of the universe, and his ways trump everything else. His plan will go forth. He will thwart our efforts, frustrate our striving, and put obstacles in the way of our efforts to be in control. We can keep fighting his plan, or we can learn to welcome his ways.

And what a beautiful plan God has for you. There is no need to fear his ways or the twists and turns he allows in your life. Like a good father, God wants what is best for his children. Your task, then, is to rest in him, to nestle into his goodness, trusting that his ways are higher and better than ours.

*Lord, thank you that your plans for
me are plans for good. Thank you for
the deep peace and joy that come
when I trust in that truth, amen.*

He saved us, not because of righteous things
we had done, but because of his mercy.

TITUS 3:5

We use the word *mercy* without truly understanding its meaning. According to Google.com, *mercy* means "compassion or forgiveness shown toward someone whom it is within one's power to punish or harm." Because we live a life of sin, choosing our own way over God's ways, we deserve judgment. And God, who dwells in brilliant light, has the authority to enact that judgment.

It's within his power and right to judge your actions along with your motivations. But Titus 3:5 reminds you of something extraordinary: God didn't save you because he felt sorry for you. Nor did he save you because you did great things to deserve it. No, he saved you from judgment solely because his nature is mercy and love.

God's very essence is compassion and forgiveness, and those traits form the basis of his mercy. This is the gift he wants to give you today and always. Whatever sin is burdening you, take note of this: God's mercy is available to you in full measure today.

Lord, I'm amazed at your mercy.
Shower me with it today, amen.

March 6

The cloud of the Lord was over the tabernacle by day, and fire was in the cloud by night, in the sight of all the Israelites during all their travels.

EXODUS 40:38

What an encouragement these tangible signs of God's presence must have been to the Israelites! Whether it was the cloud resting over the tabernacle during the day or the fire at night, the Israelites were constantly reminded of God's presence. And wherever the people traveled, taking with them the tabernacle, this evidence of God's presence accompanied them.

Today we see evidence of God's presence with us when we spend time with his people who are tabernacles of God. You may know fellow believers who overflow with God's love, who are sure sources of God's wisdom, who choose joy in the Lord that is contagious, or who have an amazing heart and giftedness for prayer. What an encouragement these people are.

And what an encouragement you can be to others as well, for you are also a tabernacle of God. He is present within you.

No matter where you travel, God is with you.

Lord, I'm grateful that you are present within me. Use me, Spirit, to draw people to God's love and his kingdom. I love you, amen.

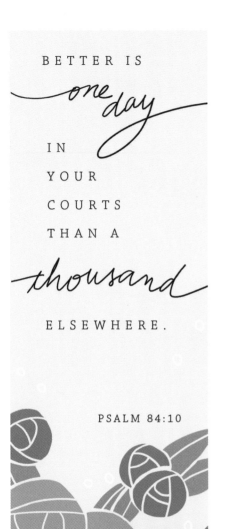

BETTER IS *one day* IN YOUR COURTS THAN A *thousand* ELSEWHERE.

PSALM 84:10

*Better is one day in your courts
than a thousand elsewhere.*

PSALM 84:10

Sometimes our most vivid memories are very simple moments that are nonetheless richly significant. A walk in the woods with a dear friend. A conversation with a child over an everyday meal. A walk down an aisle. The moment a child hollers her way into the world.

God wants us to have memorable moments with him as well. He longs for us to string together daily encounters with him, brief conversations with him, and glimpses of his presence with us that we can fondly look back on. And why not be creative as you attempt to do this?

You might create little pieces of art in response to reading the Bible. Or you might concentrate on having a continual conversation with God throughout the day. Maybe your commute can be a time to worship him in song. And maybe you'll serve the homeless on a cold night.

Spending time with Jesus in these simple but significant ways will deeply enrich your life as well as your relationship with him.

*Lord, I want to spend my day mindful
of you. Please show me how, amen.*

March 8

The man said, "The woman you put here with me—she gave me some fruit from the tree, and I ate it."

GENESIS 3:12

We can spend our lives blaming other people for our own failures. But if someone else is always the problem, we don't face our own failures and limitations. We don't grow.

Back in the garden, Adam didn't own up to his role in the original sin. Instead, he opted to point his finger at Eve. The fall of man inaugurated this blame game.

While it is true that others have hurt you, causing you tremendous pain and maybe even leading to some bad decisions on your part, we all have to stand before God alone. Even if the other person is 99 percent wrong and you are only 1 percent responsible, you will experience joy when you fess up to your part—when you confess to others and to God.

Lord, help me recognize my role, accept responsibility, apologize and/or ask forgiveness, and do my best to make the situation right. I want to avoid the blame game and instead know the joy and freedom of your design! Amen.

*We have this hope as an anchor
for the soul, firm and secure.*

HEBREWS 6:19

*E*motions dip and soar. Our days can hinge on their fickle ways. And yet, this verse promises there is security that is solid, unwavering.

You may be worried about a loved one's wanderings. Or maybe you're in financial hardship. Or perhaps your dreams have been dashed. Maybe you've lost someone dear to you through death or betrayal. In all these situations, God provides hope.

And the hope he offers isn't wishful thinking. It is based on truth and reality. We have hope for today as well as for the future because Jesus came, lived a sin-free life, died in our place, and beat death by resurrecting. That historical fact cannot be refuted.

The author of Hebrews called this hope an anchor for the soul. The waves around you may be crashing, but this hope rooted in your good God holds you in the storm. That anchor is fixed and cannot be removed. Wherever you find yourself in the storm today, choose to believe in the reality and power of this well-anchored hope.

*Lord, you are my hope. Help me remember that
when life and emotions become a storm, amen.*

March 10

We were therefore buried with him through baptism into death in order that, just as Christ was raised from the dead through the glory of the Father, we too may live a new life.

ROMANS 6:4

$\mathcal{B}$eing baptized is not only an act of obedience to God's command, but it offers a picture of the Christian life.

When we are submerged in the water, we identify with the death of Jesus. Baptism also marks that our old life has been crucified and that our sin has been gloriously removed.

When we emerge from under the waves, resurrection takes on new meaning. We couldn't breathe; now we can. We couldn't see clearly; now we can. We were near death; now we are alive.

And we are alive to a brand-new life. No matter how discouraged you may be, you are loved by God. You are renewed by the Spirit. You are alive in Jesus. With God's forgiveness of your sin an unshakeable reality, you can live with resurrection strength, perspective, and hope.

Lord, I'm grateful for the death and resurrection of baptism. Help me to truly live a brand-new life of freedom and joy, amen.

*You provide a broad path for my feet,
so that my ankles do not give way.*

2 SAMUEL 22:37

*A*t certain times in our lives we simply cannot keep walking. In those times, we desperately need to experience the rest that God has for us. We need to, for instance, experience the lovingkindness he shows by broadening a path and protecting our ankles— two things necessary for walking well and walking long.

Are you worn out? Wearied by the rat race? Stressed beyond measure?

Then perhaps it's time to slow down and ask God to both broaden your path and provide for you a time of rest. Make some time this week to be quiet and still. Then, when you have settled your mind and heart, ask God to adjust your perspective on your circumstances, to speak life where death reigns, and to encourage your weary soul.

God loves you. He wants to help you throughout your journey. And he never wearies of your prayers.

Lord, I desperately need a broad path and a day or two of deep, deep rest in you. I thank you in advance for taking care of me yet again, amen.

Make sure that nobody pays back wrong for wrong, but always strive to do what is good for each other and for everyone else.

1 THESSALONIANS 5:15

We live in a world of vigilante justice, not only on a large scale, but also in daily life. If people hurt us, we want them to be hurt too. It only seems fair.

But Paul described an entirely different way of living here. Instead of payback in kind, he highlighted *kind payback*. Instead of retaliation, we refresh. Instead of injuring, we initiate healing.

Such behavior seems impossible, especially if we've been hurt by someone. It's even harder when someone has purposefully hurt a person we love. While it's absolutely okay to pursue justice through legal means when a law has been broken, we also have to obey God's commands however painful a situation is.

Wherever you are today, ask God to give you his perspective on the situation. Ask for him to empower you to love, and be honest when you want to retaliate instead. God loves to come alongside those who long to love others but find it difficult.

Lord, I am often tempted to pay back wrong for wrong. Help me to love back instead, amen.

JOHN 15:12

*"My command is this: Love each
other as I have loved you."*

JOHN 15:12

This command is so simple, so profound,
and so hard to follow.

Maybe it will be helpful to look at exactly
how Jesus loved others. The Gospels show us
that he pursued the outcasts, let himself be
interrupted, and inconvenienced himself for
the sake of others. We see that Jesus brought
healing and grace and truth. He told stories,
sometimes shared hard truth, and always
extended an invitation to follow him.

What would it look like to love people
Jesus' way? We can pursue people who are
sitting on the outskirts of life. We can set aside
our to-do list and instead create a to-love list.
We can let someone's immediate need override our agenda. We can ask God to use us to
bring healing to the broken, grace to the legal-
istic, and truth to the confused. We can share
our own stories of God's goodness to us, and
we can share the gospel, praying that those
who listen will choose to follow Jesus.

Let's love as Jesus loved.

*Lord, use me to love others with your love
that they might love you too, amen.*

*Whoever dwells in the shelter of the Most
High will rest in the shadow of the Almighty.*

PSALM 91:1

Visitors don't dwell. Out-of-town guests don't dwell. Those whose name is on the lease or on the check that pays the mortgage dwell. Dwellers also make the beds, do the laundry, prepare the meals, love the people who share the address.

The psalmist wants you to know that same kind of daily connection to God. Make God your spiritual dwelling place and be mindful of his presence with you in your earthly dwelling. So talk to him as you make beds, do laundry, cook dinner, and love your family.

Furthermore, when you make God your dwelling place, you will find the rest you've been longing for—under God's shadow.

Are you feeling weak today? Scattered? Untethered? Does God seem far away? Invite him into the mundane of your day, trusting that he will give you both the strength and, later, the rest you need.

*Lord, I want to dwell with you today, enjoying
your presence and relying on your power, amen.*

May the Lord repay you for what you have done. May you be richly rewarded by the Lord, the God of Israel, under whose wings you have come to take refuge.

RUTH 2:12

Naomi shared this blessing with her daughter-in-law Ruth who sacrificially left her country, family, and life to join her as she returned to her homeland. Noting Ruth's extreme faith, Naomi spoke words that serve as a sweet example for us today.

First, Ruth made a choice. She *did* something. When faced between staying in the relative security of her country and following her mother-in-law to a new land, Ruth chose the latter. She risked.

Second, in making this decision, Ruth showed that she trusted God to be her refuge. Even though she was not an Israelite, she trusted in the Jewish God to protect her.

The result? Just as Naomi had prayed, God richly blessed Ruth for her choice and her trust in him.

What about you? What choice do you need to make today? What step of faith—of choosing to trust in his protection—could you, like Ruth, take?

Lord, I want to choose to trust you today. Give me the courage and faith to be like Ruth, amen.

*If anyone is in Christ, the new creation has
come: The old has gone, the new is here!*

2 CORINTHIANS 5:17

Satan would like us to think that we can never change—that we'll keep doing the same bad things or that we'll never overcome that obstacle that's held us back for years. Don't buy into his lie.

The gospel of Jesus Christ is about renewal, as is today's verse. Anyone who is "in Christ" is a new creation. You are utterly changed from who you were before you knew him. Because of the cross, God's Spirit is at work within you, making you more like Jesus. That means you can more easily choose to do the right thing, to love hard-to-love people, and to step into the purpose God has for you.

What a joy-filled truth: you are a new creation! And the reality of this newness is not based on how you act or how you feel. No, it is based on Jesus Christ, who never changes, who always loves, who always empowers. Ask him to help you live in light of your renewal today.

*Lord, remind me of the certainty of my
newness in Christ and empower me
to live in that reality today, amen.*

Love your NEIGHBOR as YOURSELF.

GALATIANS 5:14

"Love your neighbor as yourself." If you bite and devour each other, watch out or you will be destroyed by each other.

GALATIANS 5:14–15

A pack of dogs can either protect or destroy. If they cooperate with one another, they survive. If they turn on each other, they won't. They'll "bite and devour each other" to the point of death.

Paul warned us that if we spend our lives biting others (being mean, slandering, hurting people with our words or actions), we will be devoured ourselves.

The remedy for this dog-eat-dog way of living is . . . love. The remedy is to live like Jesus, who truly loved his neighbors well. It's to look out for the interests of others and place their needs before yours sometimes. And it's to choose the unchosen, to love the unlovely, to listen to the unheard.

If you've experienced dog-eat-dog living, choose differently today. Bless instead of curse. Embrace instead of shun. And if you feel you can't do these things in your strength, ask Jesus. He will gladly help you love others.

Lord, I don't want to be devoured by meanness. Instead, give me the power to love the people in my life, even those who have hurt me, amen.

I am not ashamed of the gospel, because
it is the power of God that brings
salvation to everyone who believes:
first to the Jew, then to the Gentile.

ROMANS 1:16

The gospel doesn't exclude people.

When the resurrected Jesus hung out with the astonished disciples, the question was "When are you going to restore the kingdom of Israel?"

He had spent his last three years on earth talking exclusively about the kingdom of God, how others were welcomed into it. He praised Samaritans and dignified women, and he demonstrated what outrageous love was and how open the kingdom of God is. Still, the disciples wanted to know solely about their own nation's status in the kingdom of God.

When Jesus died on the cross, his outspread arms seemed to welcome the entire world—even the Gentiles whom the Jews disdained. The crucifixion was the most surprising act of love known to man.

And that love continues today. It welcomes you into the ragtag band of Christ followers. Rest in that today.

Lord, thank you that you have invited
me into your kingdom, amen.

Follow God's example, therefore,
as dearly loved children.

EPHESIANS 5:1

*W*e can tend to camp on the first part of Paul's instruction here, and it is an important command: we who love God must follow his perfect example "and walk in the way of love, just as Christ loved us and gave himself up for us" (v. 2). But it's also important to note the *therefore* and what comes after. How are we to follow Him? "As dearly loved children."

Dearly loved children have freedom in the presence of their loving parents—freedom to live, laugh, and love.

Does this description match your approach to life? It can be easier to point to someone else and say, "Hey, you are a dearly loved child of God" than it is to declare yourself a dearly loved child of God. But that statement is absolutely true: you *are* dearly loved by your Creator.

Rest today in knowing there's nothing you can do to alter God's amazing love for you. You are dearly loved.

Lord, it's hard for me to say it, but I
am your dearly loved child. I believe;
help my unbelief, amen.

*"See, I am doing a new thing! Now it springs up;
do you not perceive it? I am making a way in
the wilderness and streams in the wasteland."*

ISAIAH 43:19

God is in the newness business. He loves to take what is broken and made it brand-new. He loves to make pathways in our lives where none existed before. He loves to pour water on our parched souls and see new growth.

But notice the question God spoke through Isaiah: "Do you not perceive it?" The implication here is that the Israelites—who were promised this new thing—might go on with their lives and miss God's renewal efforts.

And the same can happen to us. When we get caught up in the thickets of our own wildernesses, or when we focus solely on our lack, we can miss the great things God is actually doing.

You are created for blessing. God longs to make a pathway through your wilderness. He wants to water your dried ground. Respond today by simply opening your eyes and asking God to reveal to you where he is working. And then watch his glory unfold.

*Lord, I don't want to miss what you're
doing. Open my eyes, amen.*

She said to herself, "If I only touch
his cloak, I will be healed."

MATTHEW 9:21

She had been bleeding for twelve years, yet those long years had not deadened her faith. Undoubtedly anemic and weak, labeled unclean by her people, and isolated from society for more than a decade, she nevertheless approached Jesus. Destitute after spending all her money on doctors who did nothing to help her, and utterly desperate, she was banking on this itinerant Rabbi.

She didn't even consider herself worthy to touch his skin. Nevertheless—and as weak as she was—she moved toward Jesus and touched the fringe of his cloak.

Instantly, the flow of blood stopped. Instant health. Instant relief. Instant community. Jesus restored her. Instant joy.

And this can happen to you today. Whatever has you feeling desperate, dare to be like this woman and reach out for Jesus. Your desperation invites Jesus' presence, restoration, and healing.

Lord, I am tired and needy. I reach out for you
today. Hear my desperate prayer, amen.

"Enter through the narrow gate. For wide is the gate and broad is the road that leads to destruction, and many enter through it. But small is the gate and narrow the road that leads to life, and only a few find it."

MATTHEW 7:13–14

It's not easy to squeeze our way through a narrow opening. We do it to get into hidden places, or to discover something we've never seen before. Maybe we've inched our way through a cave in order to see a hidden chamber. What lies beyond the narrow opening compels us to move forward.

It's the same with our faith in Jesus. Treasures and joys await those of us who follow Jesus, but the way to those things is quite narrow. Only when we allow ourselves to become smaller will we make our way through.

It's far easier to take the wider path. But narrowing your shoulders and following Jesus to the new adventures he has for you is worth the squeezing. After all, that narrow road is the pathway to abundant life in Jesus and eternal life with him.

Lord, I want to choose the narrow path every day of my life. I know it is worth the squeezing, amen.

*Give thanks to the L*ORD*, for he is good; his love endures forever.*

PSALM 107:1

All of us have experienced fickle love. Some people we expected to love us forever ended up betraying us. Others walked away. Far away. Some outright injured us. Some were in our lives for only a season. Some who loved us were amazing blessings, but they passed away, leaving us alone. Heartbreak comes. This is a sad truth.

But here's a good truth: God's love endures forever. He will not betray. He will not walk away.

God will not injure us. Instead, he allowed his Son, Jesus, to be injured—to be crucified, to be murdered—for our sin. And God cannot die. He is eternal.

God's love never, ever falters. It's not dependent on how good you are either. No, it's dependent only on his goodness, which is also everlasting.

No matter where you find yourself today in terms of broken relationships, find rest in knowing God's love for you will last forever.

Lord, thank you for your forever love for me. I needed to hear that today, amen.

"Between us and you a great chasm has been set in place, so that those who want to go from here to you cannot, nor can anyone cross over from there to us."

LUKE 16:26

So many people don't yet know Jesus. They are living their lives as if either he doesn't exist or he does exist but his life on earth didn't matter. Not only is there a spiritual chasm between these people and God, but also there is a lack of understanding. They simply cannot fathom why Jesus came to die for us.

These people will begin to understand him when they see us live joyfully. With our infectious devotion to him, we will show what it's like to live without a chasm between us and God.

Don't be discouraged if some people in your life mock you for your devotion to Jesus. Don't grow weary in extending to them love, respect, and kindness. As you do so, you are demonstrating the reality of Jesus, the love he has that is counterintuitive. That love bridges the chasm between their hearts and God's.

Lord, I want to love others with your love. Use me so they will finally come to know you, amen.

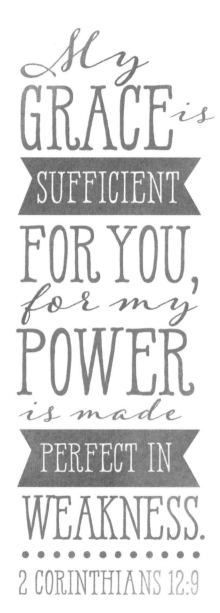

My GRACE is SUFFICIENT FOR YOU, for my POWER is made PERFECT IN WEAKNESS.

2 CORINTHIANS 12:9

[God] said to me, "My grace is sufficient for you, for my power is made perfect in weakness."

2 CORINTHIANS 12:9

By all estimations, the apostle Paul seems to have been a super-Christian. He preached throughout the Mediterranean, started churches, and wrote a big portion of the New Testament—and he survived stoning, floggings, shipwrecks, beating, hunger, and imprisonment for his faith.

We also know that Paul suffered from "a thorn in [the] flesh" that God allowed (v. 7). Scholars are uncertain what this could be. The great apostle Paul had to learn the valuable lesson that sometimes we need difficulties to keep us humble and dependent on God. Sometimes God allows these thorns so that we'll turn to him. We can be powerful —in God's strength—only when we know our weakness.

So today, if you're feeling weak and needy, if there are thorns aplenty, know that you can turn to God and receive his strength.

Lord, I am tired of being tormented by this thorn, so I choose to turn to you. I am going to rely on you to be the strength in my weakness, amen.

*"Return to your fortress, you prisoners
of hope; even now I announce that I
will restore twice as much to you."*

ZECHARIAH 9:12

What does it look like to be a prisoner of hope? You may know people who are prisoners of fear or worry or debt or painful relationships, but a prisoner of hope?

Hope is founded on God's overarching plan. He created mankind, watched them rebel, chose a nation to represent his glory, watched them rebel again, sent them into captivity, rescued them, sent his Son to die for all of us, then resurrected Jesus Christ. Our faith is based on his life, his death, and his resurrection.

Because of what Jesus did in defeating sin and death, we can become joyful prisoners of hope. We can, for instance, be bound by the hope that God has our good in mind, that today's painful situation will mean something in light of eternity, that resurrection comes after death.

For what situation in your life could you use a hefty dose of hope?

*Lord, thank you that you give me
hope for my life, and I'm grateful it's
as secure as a prison, yet gives me the
freedom of living in your love, amen.*

*Pray continually, give thanks in
all circumstances; for this is God's
will for you in Christ Jesus.*

1 THESSALONIANS 5:17-18

*M*any of us long to know God's will: Where should we live? What should we do?

But in today's Scripture, Paul stated God's will very clearly. If we do the two things Paul mentioned, we will always be doing God's will.

First, we must pray continually. We are, in other words, to maintain a continual conversation with God throughout the day.

We also are to give thanks in every situation we find ourselves in. Even when we're in pain, we look to find something beautiful, and we thank God for that. If we are facing a challenge, we thank him in advance for growing us through that difficulty.

Both these tasks—praying and giving thanks—are daily. Actually, they are to continue throughout each day. Know that as you pray and give thanks, other aspects of God will become clearer. So take some time today to pray and to practice gratitude.

*Lord, I give you every aspect and every
minute of my day. And I choose to thank
you no matter what happens, amen.*

*Do not gloat over me, my enemy! Though
I have fallen, I will rise. Though I sit in
darkness, the LORD will be my light.*

MICAH 7:8

God loves to be our light. He loves to pick us up when we fall down. He loves to comfort and defend us when he sees our enemies gloating. Why? There's a simple clue hidden within this verse. In Hebrew, the word LORD is *Yahweh*, and it means "I am that I am."

That name is significant: it means that God is the God of this moment. He existed before; he exists today; he will exist tomorrow. This truth should bring tremendous hope! Furthermore, Yahweh holds everyone's stories in his mind and their lives in his hands. He discerns everything, knows every plot twist, and is deeply concerned with every human being on this earth.

So if you find yourself in the darkness today, your mood fallen into a pit of pain, remember that God is powerful enough to see you through.

*Yahweh, thank you for being all-powerful yet
concerned about everything in my life, amen.*

*Charm is deceptive, and beauty is fleeting; but
a woman who fears the LORD is to be praised.*

PROVERBS 31:30

To charm someone means to use one's looks and wiles to achieve something—to, for instance, gain attention, take advantage of someone, or get your way. This proverb reminds us women that living by our charms will ultimately not satisfy. If we charm others— if we manipulate people into relationship with us—we will never know if they genuinely love us for who we are.

Beauty does fade with the years, and that is true for everyone. Beauty simply cannot and does not last. But the beauty of our souls is eternal, and we can cultivate that beauty if we want. A beautiful soul fears the Lord, values his opinion of her more than anyone else's, and honors him with all she thinks, says, and does. A beautiful soul serves with no regard for self, worships her God whatever the circumstances of her life, and shares openly about her heavenly Father's goodness. No wonder God is pleased and she is praised!

You will find joy in pursuing a beautiful soul.

*Lord, I ask you to make my soul
beautiful for your great glory! Amen.*

Remember the Lord, who is great and awesome,
and fight for your families, your sons and
your daughters, your wives and your homes.

NEHEMIAH 4:14

When this Scripture was penned, the Israelites were in the process of reclaiming Jerusalem, but their beloved city was without a protective wall. Imagine the fear they felt as enemies surrounded them. God's promise to them in that situation was simply this: he is awesome, and they should fight.

What battles do you face today? What "enemies" have surrounded you? Remember, nothing is too hard for God. He sees your fight, he understands your worries, and he recognizes the difficulties you face.

So, instead of despairing about what you may face today, turn afresh to God. Remember his faithfulness to you in the past. Write down details that will remind you of his great power. Stand fully in awe of him. Trust that he has everything—including your family—in his loving hands.

The truth is, you are never alone in your battles. God sees, and he will help.

Lord, sometimes my problems feel like giant
battles. Help me run to you in the midst of
them, for you are strong and mighty, amen.

YOU ARE MY SON, WHOM I LOVE, WITH YOU I AM WELL PLEASED.

MARK 1:11

A voice came from heaven: "You are my Son, whom I love; with you I am well pleased."

MARK 1:11

*I*n the wilderness of Judea, John the Baptist was "preaching a baptism of repentance for the forgiveness of sins" (v. 4). So of course he hesitated when Jesus, the sinless One, approached. Jesus didn't need to be baptized, yet he insisted: he wanted to identify in every way with the human beings he would die for.

As Jesus arose from the water, everyone heard, "You are my Son, whom I love; with you I am well pleased." Here, even before Jesus' ministry began, God affirmed his love for his Son. Already God was pleased with Jesus— pleased undoubtedly with his heart of service and sacrificial love.

Too many people today long to hear from their earthly father the words Jesus heard at his baptism. Maybe you're one of them. Maybe you have been living with that heartache, exhausting yourself trying to earn approval. Receive, then, the gift of God the Father's love for you, his adopted child (see 1 John 3:1), and trust its healing power.

Lord, help me receive your Father's love for me. Please heal wounds caused by my earthly father, amen.

April

AND WE KNOW THAT IN ALL things GOD WORKS FOR the good OF THOSE WHO LOVE HiM, WHO HAVE BEEN Called ACCORDING to His purpose

ROMANS 8:28

*And we know that in all things God works
for the good of those who love him, who
have been called according to his purpose.*

ROMANS 8:28

We read this promise that God works all things for our good, but what exactly is our good? Is it that we achieve fame? Have lots of money? Look great? Succeed in our jobs? The good that God has for us doesn't involve external factors like these. Our good involves our character.

And we can be absolutely confident that he will work all the circumstances in our lives for our good, to develop in us a more godly character. As we face trials and tribulations, we can be assured that he will use those difficulties to hone our character, to strengthen our faith, and to make us more like Christ.

What amazing grace to have God use life's pain to make us more like Jesus!

*Lord, I'm grateful that you are working in
and through my difficult circumstances.
I thank you for turning my pain today
into a stronger faith tomorrow, amen.*

You, Lord, reign forever; your throne
endures from generation to generation.

LAMENTATIONS 5:19

Nothing can make a human brain feel small like the concept of forever. The sky becomes space and extends forever! Our amazing God is eternal: He never *didn't* exist. He has always been and always will be. And he always has and always will reign. Forever.

And what security we can know when we choose to trust the God who rules forever. God has walked alongside billions of people, and he continues to. Even as he was doing that, he fashioned you in your mother's womb, and he knows you intimately. And he will know you and love you forever.

Sometimes all you need in the middle of a frustrating day is to remember the eternity of God. Your difficult day will pass. That undone relationship has the potential to be transformed. We can be confident because our God is bigger than it all.

Lord, you are a good God, a present God,
an eternal God, and I love you, amen.

The LORD is near to all who call on him.

PSALM 145:18

When we go through difficult times, we might feel that God is miles away from us. We can feel isolated when we are suffering, and the more we walk the path of pain, the farther away God seems: *Why doesn't he intervene? Why doesn't he answer prayer? Why do other people seem to have easy lives?*

But this psalm reminds us of an important truth: God does come near when we invite him to. To call on him is to cry out, to nearly beg. We may be desperate for a sense of his presence. Throughout the Psalms, though, we see that God is near to people who are broken, but far from those who are stiff-necked and proud.

You may feel God is far away. But the truth is, he is as near as your breath, as close as your prayer to him. So call on him. He wants you to live in the awareness that he walks alongside you and hurts with you. Your heavenly Father truly is intimately interested in your life.

Lord, I want you to be part of my suffering. So I call on you, thirsty for your companionship, amen.

April 4

*"Though you soar like the eagle and make
your nest among the stars, from there I
will bring you down," declares the Lord.*

OBADIAH V. 4

To better understand this Old Testament verse, we need to know who is speaking and to whom.

The speaker is Obadiah, and here he was talking about the demise of Edom, an enemy of Israel. Verse 3 of Obadiah says, "The pride of your heart has deceived you . . . you who say to yourself, 'Who can bring me down to the ground?'"

Although verses 3–4 of Obadiah are about Edom, they can serve as a warning to all of us. Pride cannot only deceive our hearts, but it also renders us vulnerable to God's judgment.

So no matter what we build or how important we try to become, we must remember that God is not impressed when we choose actions that feed our pride. Instead, God upholds those who depend on him, who see him as big and themselves as small. Pride is, essentially, thinking we're bigger—smarter, better, more important—than God. And pride will bring us down.

*Lord, every day I have many opportunities
to humble myself. In those moments, may I
choose to acknowledge your bigness, amen.*

THE BEAUTIFUL WORD DEVOTIONAL *109*

TO EACH
ONE OF US
GRACE
HAS
BEEN
GIVEN AS
CHRIST
APPORTIONED IT.
✦ ✦ ✦ ✦ ✦ ✦ ✦ ✦ ✦
EPHESIANS
4:7

*To each one of us grace has been
given as Christ apportioned it.*

EPHESIANS 4:7

*I*sn't it amazing that Jesus Christ allocates grace for you personally? He who created you chose specific, amazing traits to give to you. He also has a unique plan for your life. In other words, God gives you the expressions of his grace that enable you to best love the people in your life and serve him.

Similarly, God has given specific abilities and traits to others in the body of Christ. They, too, have been given gifts that enable them to uniquely serve the needs of others.

Maybe you feel that because you lack a certain gift—you're not skilled enough to love or serve. That's completely untrue! Every one-of-a-kind, created-by-God person is needed in his kingdom. Everyone is important; *you* are important. Yes, some gifts are used up front and center stage while others are in the background, but both kinds are essential.

Bottom line, you are the only you on this earth. Only you can touch the people in your circle. Rest in knowing Jesus has uniquely equipped you to do just that.

*Lord, help me find joy in serving with the
unique gifts you've given me, amen.*

April 6

To this you were called, because Christ suffered for you, leaving you an example, that you should follow in his steps.

1 PETER 2:21

Maybe you've been to the beach, noticed a series of footprints, and tried to put your feet in them. If so, you understand the awkwardness of trying to step right where someone else has stepped.

Yet serving as God's spokesman, Peter called us to walk the steps that Jesus walked. He didn't journey through happy tulip fields. Instead, Jesus chose to suffer for our sake. His feet must've been torn up from all the walking he did to reach many, many people.

To follow in the steps of Jesus doesn't mean walking to a literal wooden cross. It means living to serve and glorify God. One way to bring God glory is to simply pause in a given situation and ask yourself, *What would Jesus do here? Would he linger when a friend is hurting? Would he give that last bit of money to a person in need?* To follow in Jesus' steps is to become more like him through the power of the Holy Spirit. .

Jesus, I want to walk in your footsteps. Help me. Use me, transform me, amen.

You also,
like living
stones, are
being built
into a
spiritual
house.

1 Peter 2:5

You also, like living stones, are being
built into a spiritual house.

1 PETER 2:5

A house needs a proper foundation to be able to withstand all sorts of conditions. After watching home improvement television, we also know just how important good bones are to a house. You can decorate a home until you make *Fixer Upper*'s Joanna Gaines take notice, but that's wasted time and effort if the house falls down around you. Decorating a poorly built home or a house standing on a weak foundation is like putting eyelash extensions on a weasel: completely futile and worthless.

The Almighty God, however, is the perfect construction worker who is building his people into a spiritual house. He first does a lot of unseen work to ensure that our lives are built solidly on the solid foundation of Jesus Christ. The bones of God's spiritual house are prayer, fellowship, study of the Word, and obedience, and they must be securely in place. Is that true for you?

Lord, help me keep in place prayer, fellowship,
study of the Word, and obedience so that I'm
a strong bone in your spiritual house, amen.

The weapons we fight with are not the weapons of the world. On the contrary, they have divine power to demolish strongholds.

2 CORINTHIANS 10:4

This world we see is not all that it seems. The Bible, for instance, reveals that a spiritual battle continuously rages all around us. We have a very real enemy, Satan, the accuser, who has made it his mission to steal, kill, and destroy (see John 10:10).

But we can't fight the spiritual battle against Satan with earthly weapons, as Paul stated above. The only effective weapons against spiritual attack are spiritual ones. Prayer, for instance, moves the heart of God and slays dragons. Giving with joy breaks down greed and pride. Intercession (praying for others) brings peace where there was conflict. Worship ruins Satan's plans. Saying the name of Jesus silences demonic voices.

Sometimes it's hard to see the spiritual dimension of life. So today, take some time to consider that the issues you face are spiritual in nature. Set aside time to pray. Ask others to pray. Sing a worship song. You'll be fighting with spiritual weapons!

Lord, help me to boldly engage in the battle raging around me and use effectively the spiritual weapons you provide, amen.

"So do not fear, for I am with you."

ISAIAH 41:10

When life careens out of control, and you feel the weight of the chaos and fear, remember this powerful truth: God is with you.

When a friendship shifts and changes, and bitterness lurks in your heart, remember this: God is with you.

When you can't pay that bill, the creditors keep calling, and you are panicking after checking your bank balance, remember this: God is with you.

When someone slanders you regularly and no one rises to defend you, remember this: God is with you.

When old age has slowed you down and you can no longer do what you used to be able to do, remember this: God is with you.

When your dream has died, and you're struggling to feel that you have any worth at all, remember this: God is with you.

When your loved one dies, and your grief stretches beyond the starry sky, remember this: God is with you.

Do not fear, dearly loved one, for God *is* with you.

*Lord, thank you that no matter what
I am facing today, I don't need to fear
because you are with me, amen.*

I pray that out of his glorious riches
he may strengthen you with power
through his Spirit in your inner being.

EPHESIANS 3:16

*I*magine running a five-mile race. At the mile marker that reads "4.5," your leg starts to cramp, and you slow to a walk. Soon, with the cramp tightening up, you can barely walk. You can see the finish line, but you realize the only way you'll get there is by crawling. When you cry out, your best friend spies you from the finish line. She sprints toward you, pulls your arm around her shoulders, and acts as your other leg. Together, with her strength supporting your disappearing strength, you cross the finish line.

That's a picture of what God wants to do in your life today. He doesn't want you to crawl through life. Instead he wants you to cry out, to ask for help. Then you can know the "power through his Spirit in your inner being." Your Almighty God will walk with you and support you, empowering you to live the kind of life that testifies to his strength.

Lord, when I am weak, I realize I need
to find strength in you. Teach me
to live in your strength, amen.

Let everything that has breath praise the Lord.

PSALM 150:6

PSALM
150:6

The requirement is minimal. If you are alive, the psalmist said, you can praise God. (In Psalm 148 the psalmist even calls the animals to praise the Lord!) You and I praise God not simply with our lips and voices. We are able to praise him with every aspect of our being and in every moment of our lives. In fact, a life of praise will be a life well lived.

We can praise God in the midst of pain. Why? Because our compassionate God is with us and helps us endure.

We can praise God in the midst of financial worries. Why? Because, ultimately, he is our Provider who loves to supply our needs and who will do so in his perfect timing.

We can praise God in the midst of relational heartache. Why? Because Jesus experienced it when he walked this earth, and he knows how to help us through it—and he can redeem it.

God is worthy of our trust, our devotion, our commitment, and our praise.

Lord, teach me to praise you with every aspect of my being and in every moment of my life, amen.

*The testing of your faith produces perseverance.
Let perseverance finish its work so that you may
be mature and complete, not lacking anything.*

JAMES 1:3–4

If you look back on the times in your life when you grew in Christ the most, you'll typically see that the circumstances surrounding your growth weren't rainbows and ponies. No, instead you grew through the crucible of trials. James called this the "testing of your faith," but there are blessings attached to this testing.

Specifically, today's Scripture promises that if you rely on the Lord as you walk through trials, you'll receive from God the gift of perseverance. And when you let perseverance teach you to endure the challenges of life as a follower of Jesus, you will find yourself receiving three more gifts: maturity, completeness, and the abundance of life in Christ.

Perseverance, maturity, and completeness are wonderful blessings—and wouldn't it be nice if we received them as a result of happy times! That is not God's design. But there is good news to take away from this reality: the fact that growth comes with trials means that your pain is never wasted.

*Lord, when a trial comes, help me trust
that you are working in me, amen.*

April 13

To the pure, all things are pure, but to those who are corrupted and do not believe, nothing is pure. In fact, both their minds and consciences are corrupted.

TITUS 1:15

According to the Merriam-Webster Dictionary, *corrupt* means "to change (something) so that it is less pure or valuable." If we constantly slip into sin, preferring to go our own way rather than follow God's ways, we will begin to experience the corruption of our souls. In short, our souls decay and become something that is *less than*.

The opposite is gloriously true, though. When you follow Jesus, choosing him and his ways, renouncing your way of living life, you will experience the forgiveness of your sins and the cleansing of your soul.

Take a moment today to surrender. Give Jesus everything that is bothering you. Ask forgiveness for the ways and times you walk in your own strength. Tell him of your desire to have an unadulterated heart. He is faithful to answer such prayers of surrender. Oh, how he loves you and longs to set you free.

Lord, I want to be entirely devoted to you, protected from corruption and being transformed into Christlikeness, amen.

*To the Jews who had believed him,
Jesus said, "If you hold to my teaching,
you are really my disciples."*

JOHN 8:31

*T*he phrase "hold to my teaching" can also be translated *abide*. To hold to Jesus' teaching means to abide in it, to dwell there, to consistently study and practice what Jesus teaches. So Jesus' disciples aren't simply people who say they are. They are people who actively pursue Jesus, watch what he did when he walked the earth, and ask for his strength to walk in a similar way.

We all struggle with hypocrisy. We don't perfectly emulate Jesus, yet Jesus knows our hearts. He recognizes people who follow him, who have a deep longing to know him and be known by him. When we have hearts like that, he shines through us.

In what ways is Jesus asking you to abide today? Do you need to make more time to read his words? Is there someone you need to forgive? Is there a place you're supposed to serve? A ministry to support? Jesus will give you the strength to obey him.

*Jesus, I want to abide in you: I want to follow
your teaching and truly be your disciple, amen.*

*From all nations people came to
listen to Solomon's wisdom.*

1 KINGS 4:34

Wisdom was a hot commodity in Solomon's day, and that reality has not changed. We still flock to wise people, particularly when we face a big decision. The truth is, none of us knows everything there is to know. That's one reason we need one another.

After all, it's important to seek out people who are wise. Who are the Solomons in your life? Who has walked a long road of consistent obedience to God? Who has weathered life's storms with grace? Who is the kind of person you'd like to become? Take a moment today to list those people. Then pray and ask God to show you how to approach one for their counsel.

Also, become the kind of person people seek out when they need counsel. You gain wisdom by gleaning from other people's words, by reading Proverbs, and by learning from your own mistakes. It's absolutely possible, with God's help, to become someone whom people go to for wisdom.

*Lord, please place wise people in my life when
I need guidance—and make me the kind
of person people seek for wisdom, amen.*

*Then I said to them, "You see the trouble
we are in: Jerusalem lies in ruins, and its
gates have been burned with fire. Come,
let us rebuild the wall of Jerusalem, and
we will no longer be in disgrace."*

NEHEMIAH 2:17

*D*evastation comes to all of us. At times
we feel like the Israelites standing in the
midst of a very broken-down Jerusalem: we lie
in ruins, and fire has consumed us.

When that's the case, Scripture reminds
us, it is okay to grieve. Afterward comes a time
when rebuilding is necessary. That's when we
ask ourselves these questions: *What walls do I
need to build today? In what places has tragedy
torn down my resolve? Where are there breaches
in my soul? What's broken?*

This may seem utterly impossible to you.
But remember: Nehemiah didn't tell just one
Israelite to build the entire wall. No, he used
the word *us,* and you can too. You're not alone
in your rebuilding project. God loves to bless
his people with a good community to help you
rebuild what's been torn down and burned.

*Lord, please show me where my rebuilding
project should start—and then bring
people to me who will help me, amen.*

Set your minds on things above,
not on earthly things.

COLOSSIANS 3:2

Our lives are busy and full. And when we focus on that the whirlwind, our stress levels rise, and our faith shrinks. Paul reminded us of a simple cure: choose to focus our thoughts on heaven and the kingdom of God. If we let ourselves be preoccupied with eternal things, the non-eternal things will fade in importance.

Of course we should not be "so heavenly minded that we're no earthly good." But when we focus on the eternal, we actually become better equipped to love the people in our world. When we remember that God sees everything we do, even the good things we do in secret, we may find ourselves even more motivated to seek out ways to bless the world for his glory.

By setting "your mind on things above"—by focusing on Jesus and learning his ways—you'll be better equipped to love people with God's love.

Lord, today I choose to think on
heavenly things so I can be of good
use to you on this planet, amen.

April 18

*[Paul and Silas] replied [to the jailer], "Believe
in the Lord Jesus, and you will be saved."*

ACTS 16:31

It was a typical night. Had a couple new prisoners. I put 'em in stocks . . . where they sat and sang, sounding peaceful, even joyful. That was a little unusual. But things got stranger. Around midnight there was an earthquake that somehow opened all the prison doors and—I still haven't figured this out—unfastened all the inmates' chains! Escaped prisoners would mean the death penalty for me, so I drew my sword to simplify things. But the prisoner named Paul said, 'Stop! Everyone's here!'. . . . And I can't explain this either, but there was something different about that man . . . because of his relationship to God. Paul told me about Jesus. And I haven't been the same since that night. Since believing in the Lord Jesus."

What is your coming-to-faith story? Few of ours could top the jailer's story! But when we talk about who we were before we believed in Jesus as our Savior, we point to the power and joy of knowing Jesus. And when others see, they may believe as well.

*Lord, use me and my story to draw
people to belief in you, amen.*

I was given a thorn in my flesh.

2 COR. 12:7

In order to keep me from becoming
conceited, I was given a thorn in my flesh,
a messenger of Satan, to torment me.

2 CORINTHIANS 12:7

On the road to Damascus, the apostle Paul was blessed with a vision of Jesus, and he committed himself to Jesus. Subsequently, Paul was blessed with a powerful and effective ministry as preacher, teacher, apologist, New Testament writer, church planter, and church leader. So, Paul said, God allowed a messenger of Satan—a "thorn in [his] flesh"—to keep him humble. Three times Paul asked God to remove the thorn, and God said no.

God then explained to Paul that his grace would enable him to cope. He introduced to Paul the kingdom paradox that when we are weakest, we are strongest.

That's because when we are weak, we turn to God, and he gives us his power.

Are you tormented by a thorn right now? Have you asked God to remove it only to hear no? Then look to him for the grace of his strength: when you are weak, God will provide you with his strength that is far stronger than your own.

Lord, thank you that in my weakness
I experience your strength, amen.

*Grow in the grace and knowledge of our
Lord and Savior Jesus Christ. To him be
glory both now and forever! Amen.*

2 PETER 3:18

The Spanish phrase *Vaya con Dios*—literally, "Go with God"—is a lovely parting thought for people to share as they go their own ways. And that thought is actually quite similar to the meaning behind *good-bye*. Did you know that *good-bye* is shorthand for "God be with you"? What an uplifting and encouraging farewell!

Peter certainly seemed a proponent of uplifting and encouraging final words. In his second letter to early believers, he wrote, "Grow in the grace and knowledge of our Lord and Savior Jesus Christ," pointing to what's most important in life: nurturing our relationship with Jesus. Then Peter added, "To him be glory both now and forever!" recalibrating an earthly perspective by lifting listeners' eyes to the Lord, the King of kings, who will reign forever.

At the end of a conversation, *good-bye* certainly works. But sometimes "God be with you!" and even "Grow in grace—and to God be the glory!" would indeed be a blessing.

*Lord, teach me to bless people with my
words at the beginning, middle, and
end of our conversations, amen.*

"Whoever wants to be my disciple must deny themselves and take up their cross daily and follow me."

LUKE 9:23

Anything worth having, costs.

Cars and houses cost. So does a college education. And so do relationships. In friendship, parenting, and marriage, we give up some of our preferences, we learn to compromise, and we often allow the other person's needs and desires to be more important to us than our own. And we do that in our relationship with Jesus too.

We pray for Jesus' will to be done on this earth. We give control of our lives over to him. Jesus called this kind of cost "denying ourselves." We deny our wishes and our will, yielding to his wishes and his will for us, trusting that his plans are better than ours. Such self-denial reflects our godly submission to the One we call Lord. Such self-denial involves following Jesus' teachings and his example, being willing to experience rejection and possibly death for him. We commit to following Jesus' teachings and example even though the cost may be high.

But anything worth having, costs.

Lord, thank you for denying yourself and giving your life for my salvation, amen.

"Look, I am coming soon! My reward is with me, and I will give to each person according to what they have done."

REVELATION 22:12

We learn three things in this verse: Jesus is coming soon. He has rewards. He will reward us based on what we have done for him on earth.

In light of eternity, Jesus' return is imminent. Although many have felt that Jesus could come back in their lifetime, we still live with joyful anticipation of his coming back and making everything right again. But even if he doesn't come back in your lifetime, you will eventually see the end of the age when justice reigns.

In the meantime, we live in the amazing truth that Jesus saved us not just so we could rest in that salvation. Jesus saved us for a purpose: to further the kingdom of God and bring light into dark places. And he notes whenever we do so, even those tasks no one sees. May you find joy in being his light!

Lord, I live in the joyous truth that you will come and justice will reign. As I await that glorious moment, may I please you and honor you in the way I live each day, amen.

The Lord is with us. Do not be afraid of them.

NUMBERS 14:9

Joshua and Caleb reported the richness of the promised land, yet the people were afraid to enter it. Joshua and Caleb saw the beauty of the land and described it as "flowing with milk and honey" (v. 8). The ten other spies, however, ignored the blessings and concentrated instead on the people too strong to conquer. Joshua encouraged the nation of Israel to enter the land God had promised them, but the Israelites were too afraid.

Maybe you feel like the Israelites. Maybe you see your problems as giants that cannot be conquered and that are bigger than what God can handle. When that is your perspective, you are exercising your worry muscle. But when you instead ask God for help, you are exercising your faith muscle and making it stronger. As a result, you also begin to see the good things God has for you where before you had seen only giants.

Worry and fear can prevent you from seeing the good. So when you sense worry or fear encroaching, turn your heart away from the giants and look to God.

Lord, please help me have faith in your ability to rescue me, amen.

April 24

"I have loved you with an everlasting love; I
have drawn you with unfailing kindness."

JEREMIAH 31:3

Have you heard it said that you can catch more flies with honey than with vinegar? This is true in the spiritual realm as well: God's sweet love is far more attractive to nonbelievers than vinegar.

And it's God's kindness that leads us toward him, and his eternal, never-ending love keeps us near. When we fail, when we sin, when we fall down, God does not shun us or rebuke us with "I warned you." Instead, he lovingly pulls us out of miry pits, sets our feet back on solid ground, and sings songs of deliverance over us. What a loving God!

God's love and kindness also are examples that can help us love our families and friends. It's important to remember that we draw people toward us not through our judgment or a harsh "I told you so," but through our kindness and compassion. Oh, to be as loving and kind as God is when we interact with those we love!

Lord, thank you for loving me so well—
and help me love people in my life
with that kind of love, amen.

Blessed are you who are poor, for yours is the kingdom of God.

LUKE 6:20

"Blessed are you who are poor, for yours is the kingdom of God."

LUKE 6:20

Throughout his teaching ministry, Jesus said things that perplexed the day's religious leaders. Some of his statements are puzzling even today.

Consider "Blessed are you who are poor." When we look at the poor, the last thing we think is how blessed they are.

But when Jesus said that the poor are blessed—and that the very kingdom of God belongs to them—he was referring to a spiritual poverty. Spiritually poor people realize they don't have the capability to better themselves in their own power. Perhaps hitting rock-bottom emotionally in life made them realize their need for Someone stronger to depend on.

We can't always save ourselves from life's tough circumstances, and we sinful human beings can never save ourselves from our spiritual dilemma of separation from a holy God. When we acknowledge our spiritual poverty, and choose dependence on God, we are humbly entering the kingdom of God.

Lord, in you and only in you, we—who know our great need for a Savior and who know you as that Savior—are rich. Help us live humbly dependent on you, amen.

You will keep in perfect peace those whose minds are steadfast, because they trust in you.

ISAIAH 26:3

The Merriam-Webster Dictionary defines *steadfast* as being "very devoted or loyal to a person, belief, or cause." It also means to be unchanging in our commitment. The Hebrew word for that kind of covenantal, longsuffering love is *hesed*. God not only models both *hesed* and steadfastness, but he wants us to become steadfast in our devotion to him. He isn't asking from us, though, what he hasn't already demonstrated for us and extended to us.

When we practice steadfastness in our love for God we please him. We also find ourselves in a place to be blessed with God's peace, with his *shalom*. This kind of peace is complete: it is knowing peace in our bodies, our minds, our spirits, and our hearts.

One more thing. The last word in today's verse is *trust*. We honor God when we trust him. So whatever you are facing today, you can choose to trust Him. Shalom.

Lord, strengthen my devotion to you, keep me steadfast in my commitment, and bless me, I pray, with your perfect peace, amen.

MY FATHER will HONOR the ONE who SERVES ME.

JOHN 12:26

"My Father will honor the one who serves me."
JOHN 12:26

Our culture tends to honor people who serve themselves, who, for instance, climb to the top of the corporate ladder without caring about whom they step on to get there. Ours is a world of self-serving people, and our culture rewards selfishness. .

So when Jesus talked to his disciples (and to us) about serving him, Jesus was issuing a countercultural mandate. He was telling us to not step on others, not see people as obstacles, and not serve ourselves.

Instead, we are to serve Jesus who modeled such service for us. He didn't come to be served; he came to serve others. He chose to consider other people as more important than himself. He washed feet. He listened to people. He valued the downtrodden and accepted them.

As you follow in Jesus' steps—as you honor him by serving others—Jesus will honor you. Now, though, savor the fact that you are pleasing your Lord and glorifying him with your selflessness, your obedience, and your servant's heart.

Lord, show me each day whom to serve, enable me to serve well, and may you receive the glory, amen.

Your name will no longer be Jacob, but
Israel, because you have struggled with God
and with humans and have overcome.

GENESIS 32:28

*I*t can be easy to think that the heroes of the faith never did anything wrong and never questioned God. A look at Jacob's life shows us otherwise. He was a conniver and a deceiver; he didn't always honor God with his life. And in Genesis 32 he wrestled with God all night long.

Such wrestling with God shouldn't surprise us. Jacob is human, and questioning is human. Having questions about your faith—wrestling with God over certain issues—doesn't deny you the privilege of being in his presence. On the contrary, wrestling with God actually means you care enough about your relationship with him that you'll engage him. Besides, God is not shaken by your questions.

Whether you wrestle with him often or easily nestle into his presence, God welcomes you with open arms.

Lord, thank you that you will wrestle with
me so I can know you better. Amen.

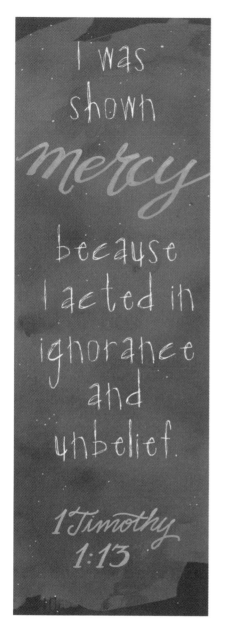

I was shown *mercy* because I acted in ignorance and unbelief.

1 Timothy 1:13

*Even though I was once a blasphemer
and a persecutor and a violent man,
I was shown mercy because I acted
in ignorance and unbelief.*

1 TIMOTHY 1:13

*B*efore he met Jesus in a dramatic way on his way to Damascus, Paul (then Saul) had made it his mission to stop the early Christian church. He stood by watching and was pleased as the Christ-follower Stephen breathed his last and then "began to destroy the church" (Acts 8:3). "Breathing out murderous threats against the Lord's disciples," Paul dragged people to prison (Acts 9:1)—until he met Jesus.

And Jesus changed Paul completely, transforming him from persecutor to humble follower. At that initial meeting, Paul melted under the mercy of Jesus, and he gave his life in service to the One he had disdained.

Think about life before you knew Jesus. You were living in your own strength, in ignorance of God's freeing truth, and enslaved to sin. Yet in the midst of such rebellion, God showed you mercy. And he continues to transform you just as he transformed Paul.

*Lord, may I be clay in your hands as you make
me more like your Son, my Savior, amen.*

He who did not spare his own Son, but gave
him up for us all—how will he not also, along
with him, graciously give us all things?

ROMANS 8:32

God made the supreme sacrifice on your behalf when he sent his Son to die for your sins. The love that compelled that gift of his Son further compels him to bless you with even more. Not only are your sins forgiven, but you also are granted a brand-new life. You are healed and given hope and joy.

Look at your life today.

What traits do you need to live in a way that glorifies and honors God? Do you need more patience? Greater trust in God? Less worrying? Know that God loves to answer your prayers. He loves to give good gifts to you. He will grow in you the traits you're longing for when you ask him.

Now consider whom you need to forgive, but are struggling to. Ask God to enable you to forgive as he has forgiven you. He will help you.

Lord, thank you that you generously
give good gifts. Your only Son to die on
my behalf and your gracious forgiveness
were just the beginning! Thank you!

May

Dear friends, since God so loved us,
we also ought to love one another.

1 JOHN 4:11

"Since God so loved us . . ." Don't skip over that remarkable statement! God loves us, and we see his absolute and unconditional love in the cross. God sent his Son to die for our sins so we could be set free from the penalty of sin and live in relationship with him forever.

Having been loved so lavishly—Jesus died for us!—we gratefully find ourselves loving God in return. His plan is for his love to then flow through us to others, and why wouldn't that happen! After all, God's love freed us, healed us, and transformed us. What a life-changing message to share with others so that they might experience the same!

But some of us get stuck: we struggle to receive God's love. Maybe we feel we don't deserve it, or that it's for other, better people, that it's too good to be true, that it's a flat-out lie. But God absolutely does love you. Ask him to help you believe. He wants you to rest in his affection, forgiveness, and love today and always.

Lord, thank you for loving me so I
can love others well, amen.

*"If you, then, though you are evil, know
how to give good gifts to your children,
how much more will your Father in heaven
give good gifts to those who ask him!"*

MATTHEW 7:11

Think back to the Christmas when you received a longed-for gift. Perhaps in that moment, you understood that your parents had sacrificed joyfully to be able to give you what you wanted. Your smile and gratitude were worth their effort. Why? Because parents naturally want to give good gifts to their children.

God is the same way. He loves to give you good gifts. These aren't under-the-Christmas-tree gifts. In fact, these gifts—things like patience, a reconciled relationship, a heart made whole after emotional trauma, unexpected provision, clear direction, his presence with you—are a million times better than anything even the best earthly parent could wrap up and put a bow on.

Almighty God is a good Father who longs to give you so much. Don't hesitate to ask, believing that he hears you and that he will give you good gifts in his perfect timing.

*Lord, I know you are the wise and perfect
parent, and I thank you that you only
give me what is good for me, amen.*

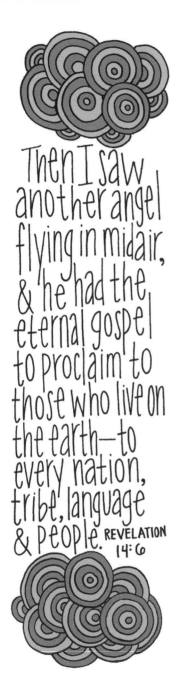

*Then I saw another angel flying in midair,
and he had the eternal gospel to proclaim
to those who live on the earth—to every
nation, tribe, language and people.*

REVELATION 14:6

*E*ventually, at the end of time, every knee on earth will bow and every tongue will confess that Jesus is Lord. People from every tribe, language, and nation will worship in joyful unity before the throne of God. Personal differences and reasons for international strife will no long matter, eclipsed by the glorious Lord we can't help but worship.

And this is possible because Jesus died on the cross for every single human being, no matter how rich or poor, no matter what color their skin is or what language they speak. Jesus welcomes everyone into his kingdom. Imagine what it will be like to hear the praises of God proclaimed in thousands of different tongues!

And someday you will be part of this heavenly choir, praising Jesus wholeheartedly and with a joy far greater than you could ever have imagined.

*Lord, I love this picture of heaven, of
all your people throughout time and
around the globe praising you with joyful
abandon! Come quickly, I pray, amen.*

*"Very truly I tell you, it is for your good
that I am going away. Unless I go away,
the Advocate will not come to you;
but if I go, I will send him to you."*

JOHN 16:7

When Jesus spoke these almost-last words to his disciples, they did not fully understand. How could it be good that he would leave them?

Jesus was talking to his disciples about the Holy Spirit when he referred to the Advocate, a word that means mediator and defender. The disciples were no doubt distraught that Jesus, whom they perceived as their Mediator, would be leaving them.

And Jesus was in fact the ultimate mediator between sinful human beings and our holy God. But the Spirit does much more for us. In Acts, we see how powerfully the Spirit came upon all of the disciples, transforming these timid followers into bold preachers and enabling them to do great things for God. This same Holy Spirit lives within you and me, empowering us to also do the great things for God that he calls us to do.

*Lord, thank you for your Spirit who
is my advocate, comforter, helper,
companion, and counselor, amen.*

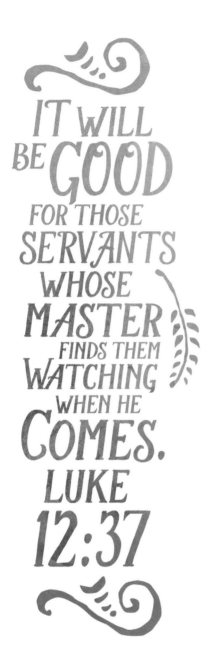

IT WILL BE GOOD FOR THOSE SERVANTS WHOSE MASTER FINDS THEM WATCHING WHEN HE COMES. LUKE 12:37

"It will be good for those servants whose master finds them watching when he comes."

LUKE 12:37

And it would be bad, Jesus went on, for the servant who decided it would be awhile before the master returned and started beating his fellow servants and drinking with the drunkards. Like these servants, we don't know when our Master—when Jesus—will return.

Jesus desires that, while we wait for his return, we work hard, being good stewards of what he has entrusted us to. This is a sharp rebuke for people who receive Christ but then forget they ever knew him. Soon they become lethargic toward spiritual things. They stop worshipping Christ.

Except that every single one of us will someday meet Jesus face-to-face. Then we will report what we did during our waiting period, that time between meeting Jesus and dying. And what exactly are you doing?

Jesus has gifted you to handle certain things for the kingdom. He has planned specific tasks that only you can perform. Your diligence in doing these will be a gift you give him in eternity.

Lord, I don't want to be spiritually lazy; I want to serve you wholeheartedly! Amen.

There are different kinds of gifts, but the same Spirit distributes them. There are different kinds of service, but the same Lord. There are different kinds of working, but in all of them and in everyone it is the same God at work.

1 CORINTHIANS 12:4–6

We've heard the statement *God works in mysterious ways.* One amazing aspect of that truth is that he uses us to work his ways in the world. Each and every believer is endowed with spiritual gifts, completely unique, utterly them-shaped.

But what happens when we dismiss our own gifts as unimportant? And why is it wrong to envy another person's gift? Those two questions have the same answer: God's Spirit is the distributor of the gifts, and when we question why we did or didn't get certain gifts, we are questioning God and his generosity.

There's only one you on this planet. And God has uniquely gifted you to reach the circle of people he has put you in. So shine there. Use the gifts God has given you and celebrate how the Lord uses you in his kingdom.

Lord, thank you for giving me specific me-shaped gifts. Help me to use them today to bless others, amen.

I cannot carry all these people by myself;
the burden is too heavy for me.

NUMBERS 11:14

*M*oses boldly spoke these very honest words to the Lord: the Israelites were far too big a burden for Moses to bear. God responded to Moses' weariness by assigning additional people to carry the load, specifically seventy elders who could help Moses lead. God heard the cry of Moses and acted.

Many of us carry burdens, and the biggest burden we may find ourselves carrying is people with all their burdens.

Did you know that God didn't design us to carry even our own burdens? We are to give our cares and concerns to the Lord. So why do so many of us spend our lives carrying not only our burdens but also the burdens of others? You don't have to.

Know that God sees you just as he saw Moses. God hears your cries. The Almighty God will carry your burden and relieve you of the heavy burdens that you are carrying for others. Let him—with relief and gratitude.

Lord, I'm weary. I'm so tired of my own
burdens and from my burdens, and I
can barely handle the weight of other
people's problems. Help me! Amen.

*Through Jesus, therefore, let us continually
offer to God a sacrifice of praise—the fruit
of lips that openly profess his name.*

HEBREWS 13:15

Sacrifice involves inconvenience. So to offer a sacrifice of praise, for instance, you are deliberately choosing to praise God rather than doing other pursuits. You're making time to worship him, to tell him how marvelous and amazing he is.

The author of Hebrews encouraged us to offer a sacrifice of praise continually. He didn't mean to sing our way through the day. Instead, the writer meant that we choose to be continually mindful of God's goodness. We don't merely thank him for the food in front of us, but we live with gratitude, thanking him for limbs that work, ears that hear, people to love.

And this praise is not simply a mental exercise. This praise involves verbal proclamation, "the fruit of [our] lips."

So, if you're having a difficult day, say out loud to the Lord, "I love you, God, and I appreciate you." It'll make a difference!

*Lord, I choose right now to openly and joyfully
praise you for who you are—and I ask you to
teach me to praise you continually, amen.*

My HELP comes from the LORD

PSALM 121:2

I lift up my eyes to the mountains—where does my help come from? My help comes from the LORD, the Maker of heaven and earth.

PSALM 121:1-2

A quick geography lesson will help us better understand this psalm.

Palestine is a mountainous land, and Jerusalem sits on top of a hill. There God made his presence known first in the tabernacle and then in the temple. In that setting, as he walked up toward Jerusalem, the psalmist praised God. The psalmist knew that mountains and hills don't—can't!—save us, but that our powerful God will help when we need him.

Do you doubt God's power? His is the power of creation as well as protection and deliverance. Look around you. He made every mountain, stream, ocean, bird, fish, animal, domesticated and wild, as well as air, water, and every other thing that exists.

This Creator God also made you, and he absolutely loves you. While you may feel as small and insignificant as a molehill, your mountain-forming God loves you and will protect and deliver you.

*Lord, I lift my eyes to you with confidence in your strength and your faithfulness...
and gratitude for your goodness
and your protection, amen.*

*We also glory in our sufferings, because we
know that suffering produces perseverance;
perseverance, character; and character, hope.*

ROMANS 5:3–4

*M*ost people glory in their accomplishments, resumes, pedigrees, or the letters after their names. But Paul gloried in his sufferings—and that is definitely countercultural kingdom thinking. It's the absolute opposite of what the world values.

Why would anyone in his right mind glory in suffering? Shouldn't we avoid suffering?

Paul knew, though, that ease never produces good character traits. Unfortunately, we only grow through pain. And Paul identified some of the growth that results: we develop perseverance, character, and hope when we suffer and invite Jesus into that suffering.

While you shouldn't chase after suffering, you can change your perspective when it arrives on your doorstep. With wisdom, you can welcome suffering as an opportunity for significant spiritual growth and character development. Ask God today to reframe the way you view suffering. Ask him to teach you what it means to glory in it.

*Lord, I need a change in my perspective
on the suffering in my life. Give me
your perspective, I pray, amen.*

FOR the SON of MAN came to SEEK and to SAVE the lost.

LUKE 19:10

"For the Son of Man came to seek and to save the lost."

LUKE 19:10

Have you ever thought about the fact that whatever you've lost is always in the last place you look? True—because then we stop looking, right? Similarly, Jesus stops looking only after he finds the one he seeks.

Jesus, for instance, had noticed Zacchaeus —the tax collector, the sinner—and invited himself to this wealthy man's home. The people who heard Jesus' plan began muttering: Jesus was going to a sinner's house? Aware of their self-righteousness, Jesus explained that he had come "to seek and to save the lost."

Zacchaeus was definitely lost: this Jewish traitor worked on behalf of Rome and stole from his own people by requiring them to pay more taxes than Rome did. Yet when Jesus entered his life, Zacchaeus became unlost, repenting of his sin and promising to pay back four times what he had wrongly taken.

Jesus went to Zacchaeus when he was lost. And he will go to your loved ones who are lost. When he finds them, he'll rejoice in their salvation as he did in yours.

Lord, thank you that you sought me when I was lost in my sin and rescued me.

"Do not be afraid of those who kill the body but cannot kill the soul. Rather, be afraid of the One who can destroy both soul and body in hell."

MATTHEW 10:28

We tend to live in fear, particularly fear of death. But in this verse Jesus reminded us that ultimately the only One we should fear is God.

And when we spend our energy and time thinking about him, learning how to please him and choosing to worship him, suddenly our fears grow smaller. The bigger we make God, the tinier our fears about life in this fallen world become.

And this God who loves with an infinite love, loves you. Right where you are. In this moment. Furthermore, nothing you can do will ever separate you from his deep fatherly affection for you. May choosing to revere him become a delight. And as you worship him— and him alone—among the byproducts will be a life without fear of death.

Lord, when my fears feel big, remind me
that you are big, that you are bigger!
Show me your greatness afresh, amen.

[Love] always protects, always trusts,
always hopes, always perseveres.

1 CORINTHIANS 13:7

When you own something of value, you protect it. You get your car's oil changed. You fix your home's leaky roof.

Similarly, when you love someone, you *protect* that person. You guard her reputation by not gossiping. You comfort her when she's hurting. You nurse her back to physical health.

Today's verse about love adds to this beautiful portrait. Love always trusts. If you love someone, you will naturally believe him or her. You'll extend the benefit of the doubt instead of jumping to conclusions.

Love always hopes. Even when a friend is far from God and making poor choices, you continue to have vigilant hope. You don't give up believing that hearts and circumstances can change because of God's great power.

Love always perseveres. You walk with someone you love no matter how rough the path. You speak words of truth and life. You're there when the one you love hits rock bottom.

And this is the kind of love Jesus has for you.

Lord, I want to love with a love
that protects, trusts, hopes and
perseveres. Please help me, amen.

May 14

"Keep my decrees and laws, for the person who obeys them will live by them. I am the Lord."

LEVITICUS 18:5

*I*n order to keep the laws, a citizen must first know the laws. And this is true for us as we follow God. We must be aware of the laws of God. They are clearly spelled out in the Ten Commandments in the Old Testament; in the New Testament Jesus summarized them for us: "Love God; love others."

But merely knowing the laws doesn't mean automatic obedience. Instead we need a new heart, a new willingness to obey, as well as the strength the Holy Spirit gives us. The Old Testament shows us how futile it is to try to keep the law in our own strength. Left on our own, we sin—a lot.

Thankfully, this promise in Leviticus is fulfilled in Jesus Christ. His life, death, and resurrection mean God regards us as righteous. Jesus' gift of the Holy Spirit means we are empowered to obey God's commands. May we do exactly that!

Lord, thank you for empowering me to live a life worthy of you—a life characterized by peace, obedience, and love, amen.

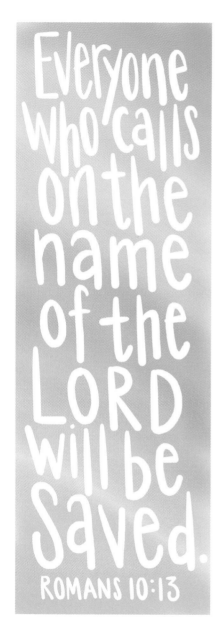

Everyone who calls on the name of the LORD will be saved.
ROMANS 10:13

Everyone who calls on the name
of the LORD will be saved.

ROMANS 10:13

What a far-reaching promise from God! Not *some* of the people. Not *the select few* who are pious enough. Not the *popular* crowd. Everyone!

But what exactly does it mean to call on the name of the Lord? Name is synonymous with nature or character. So when we call upon the Lord's name, we are calling upon his character.

And the character of Jesus was spotless, sinless. He was perfect,—to the point of dying on the cross for us "while we were still sinners" (Romans 5:8).

Just as the word *everyone* brings deep comfort, so do the words *will be*. The apostle Paul was making a definitive statement: salvation was sure—and not because of anything you did but because of Jesus' death and resurrection. Even if you feel beaten down or totally unworthy of God's rescue of you from the consequences of your sin, the truth is, you are saved because of God's faithfulness and grace.

Lord, you are gracious and forgiving,
and I thank you for saving me from the
eternal consequences of my sin, amen.

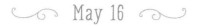

May 16

*I know that my redeemer lives, and that
in the end he will stand on the earth.*

JOB 19:25

You may be familiar with these words as lyrics to a popular Christian hymn. But consider who first said these words—Job, a man described as "blameless and upright" but who had everything taken away from him (Job 1:8).

So many times we blame God when things go wrong. The last thing we want to do is make faith-filled statements about him when we feel abandoned. But Job gives us an amazing example to follow. He shifted his focus from his circumstances and sorrows, and he fixed his eyes on his redeemer.

Your redeemer *does* live. He *will* stand on this earth, victorious over sin and death. That truth should usher in a heap of joy and peace. You may be facing worry and stress, but you can choose to focus on the reality of God's ever-present power for you and the eternal life he has for you. He is victorious. And because he lives, you will too.

*Lord, I want to focus on you, my redeemer,
who lives! I want to live in light of your
victory over sin and death, amen.*

Whoever does not love does not know God, because God is love.

1 JOHN 4:8

Through the centuries, people have said and done all sorts of evil in the name of God. According to this verse, that doesn't make sense because God's nature is love. His very essence is love. His modus operandi is love. God is love.

So if someone is speaking or acting hatefully but proclaiming Jesus, something's not right. Such hatred indicates no genuine knowledge of the one true God.

How did Jesus deal with those who hated? He rebuked them harshly, but he also demonstrated a better way to live. When, for instance, he could have rightfully wiped out all the people involved in his crucifixion, when he could have summoned legions of angels to rescue him, he chose something quite different; He asked that God would forgive them. He recognized that they didn't know what they were doing. He loved them.

This same ability to love and forgive your enemies is within you through the power of the Holy Spirit. Calling on him, you can love others, however wrong their treatment of you, and demonstrate God's outrageous love.

*Lord, I need your Spirit to help
me love and forgive, amen.*

Keep this Book of the Law always on your lips; meditate on it day and night, so that you may be careful to do everything written in it. Then you will be prosperous and successful.

JOSHUA 1:8

To keep God's Word on our lips, we need to know it and immerse ourselves in it. That means reading it, memorizing it, and thinking about it—or, to use Joshua's word, meditating on it.

But what exactly does it mean to meditate on Scripture? One very simple way is the practice of *Lectio Divina* ("divine reading"). Take a passage and read it out loud. Ask God to speak to you through its words. Stop to listen. Pray. Then read through the passage a second time, then a third, asking God to give you deeper insight each time.

Another great practice is to simply write out Scripture. Find a simple journal; then write out your favorite passages, asking God to cement those words in your heart as you put them on the page.

Lord, I want to know your Word, not just intellectually, but in my soul. And I want my life to reflect my knowledge of it, amen.

THE LORD WHO RESCUED ME FROM THE PAW OF THE LION AND THE PAW OF THE BEAR WILL RESCUE ME FROM THE HAND OF THIS PHILISTINE.

1 SAMUEL 17:37

The LORD who rescued me from the paw of the lion and the paw of the bear will rescue me from the hand of this Philistine.

1 SAMUEL 17:37

Everything that's happened to us in the past prepares us to face our giants today. David recounted his own escapades with wild things and God's faithfulness) as he faced the wildest one of all: Goliath.

If you're facing a giant, take a few minutes to recount the many times God has rescued you. Look back on your life and note the places God intervened. When did he come to your aid? When was a relationship salvaged? A job renewed? A financial situation stabilized?

When you remember amazing things God has done and remind yourself of his faithfulness, you are better able to face whatever giant looms before you. Remember, God is bigger than giants. He is bigger than circumstances. He is bigger than your problems. Furthermore, he can be trusted, and he loves to help you.

Lord, help me remember that you are faithful and that you are bigger than the giants I face, amen.

*Since we have now been justified by
his blood, how much more shall we be
saved from God's wrath through him!*

ROMANS 5:9

*W*e don't speak much about God's wrath these days. We prefer to talk about his love. But we must understand God's wrath in order to better grasp the depth of his love.

We are naturally sinners, unable to make ourselves holy, and that is the requirement for entering God's presence. As sinners, then, we were without hope. Sin is so terrible that it takes a blood sacrifice to cover over it, to usher in forgiveness. So God sent Jesus as a once-and-for-all sacrifice. His blood paid the price for everyone's sin—everyone in the whole world, including you.

Jesus satisfied God's requirement of holiness by living a sinless life. Then, as the spotless Lamb, Jesus died: he was the blood sacrifice that God's Law required. And Jesus' death ushered us into the era of grace. God welcomes us into relationship with him because of Jesus' shed blood. What a Savior!

*Lord, I don't know how to thank you for
dying for me, for shedding your blood on my
behalf. But I am so grateful you did, amen.*

"In the same way, I tell you, there is rejoicing in the presence of the angels of God over one sinner who repents."

LUKE 15:10

Jesus told of a shepherd who leaves his ninety-nine sheep to find the one that has gone astray. This shepherd's action reveals Jesus' heart and his desire that no one would perish but find everlasting life through him. And when someone does come to him—or when he is able to carry a lost lamb home—angels rejoice!

Many of us have loved ones who are that one lost sheep. And perhaps all you can do is pray. Know that that can be enough!

A simple reminder to pray is to grab a pen, write 99/1 on a sticky note, and put it in a prominent place. Every time you see it, those numbers will remind you of Jesus' determination to chase after the one.

One more thing: when you worry about your friend or family member who is far from God, think about your own story. Remember how God pursued you, and rest there.

Lord, I am so thankful that no one is too far from your reach. Please bring my loved one into your flock, I pray, amen.

*When the angel of the LORD appeared
to Gideon, he said, "The LORD is
with you, mighty warrior."*

JUDGES 6:12

Gideon was an unlikely hero. He didn't qualify—at least in his mind—as someone whom God would use in his plan. But God called Gideon "mighty warrior." Clearly, God saw something in Gideon that he couldn't see in himself.

Do you realize that God also sees in you abilities and giftedness that you don't? You may know your weaknesses aplenty. Yet God sees your potential. Why? He knows what can happen when his strength works through your weakness.

God loves to choose humble individuals to do extraordinary tasks because he knows he will get the glory. So instead of feeling disqualified for whatever God calls you to in life, reach for him. Ask for his strength. Have faith in his ability to make you able. That's when you begin to see God work in your life.

*Lord, thank you that you see me as a
mighty warrior. I know I can accomplish
what you want me to accomplish
because of your strength in me, amen.*

On my bed I remember you; I think of you through the watches of the night.

PSALM 63:6

The watches of the night were military time periods—from dusk to 10:00 p.m., 10:00 p.m. to 2:00 a.m., and 2:00 a.m. to dawn—indicating the shifts when soldiers kept watch over the nation and the temple. These could be lonely periods of time when the soldier had to fight off sleep and stay extremely alert in case predators or enemies came near.

David, the author of this psalm, was a soldier and therefore familiar with such a military assignment. Even if he never served as a sentry, he knew of the duty and referred to it as he lay restless, sleepless, this night. In his wakefulness, David chose to think about God and pray to him.

The next time you have a wakeful night, follow David's example. Turn a night of tossing and turning into an opportunity to be with your God. Praise him and pray to him. Rest in his presence.

God will meet you in those quiet moments. In fact, he keeps watch over you all through the night, every night.

Lord, thank you for keeping watch over me and over my family, amen.

*Do not be stiff-necked, as your
ancestors were; submit to the Lord.*

2 CHRONICLES 30:8

To be stiff-necked is to be stubborn. It's making the choice to only do things our way, without advice or assistance from anyone else. Basically, stiff-necked people act as if they know everything there is to know about a situation.

No one likes hanging out with a stiff-necked individual. There is no real interaction, no two-way communication

The Lord doesn't want us to be stiff-necked. He wants us to realize that we don't know everything there is to know about our lives. He wants us to be different from the Israelites who went their own way again and again—and always ended up in a heap of trouble.

God's instruction to the stiff-necked and to you and me is simple: submit. To submit is to acknowledge that God is God and you are not, that his ways are better than yours. A submissive believer actively seeks God's counsel and then does what God says to do.

So, where are you on the stiff-necked meter today?

*Lord, I don't want be stiff-necked! Instead, I
choose today to submit to you in everything—
and I ask you to help me, amen.*

WHAT *good* IS IT *for* SOMEONE *to* gain THE WHOLE WORLD, *yet* FORFEIT *their* soul ?

MARK 8:36

"What good is it for someone to gain the whole world, yet forfeit their soul?"

MARK 8:36

Money can buy temporary happiness in a variety of forms, but it cannot buy eternal life. Yet for many people in pursuit of the almighty dollar, eternity is not even on their minds. They focus their thoughts and their hearts on wealth. They are no longer serving God. As Jesus said, we human beings either serve God, or we serve money.

The enemy of our souls would like us to concentrate on the here and now, on what can make us happy, and money is a great tool for that short-term satisfaction. When we fall for Satan's schemes, we easily forget that how we live here on earth matters for eternity.

So instead of pursuing the illusion of security that financial wealth offers, consider pursuing the eternal God who loves you and died for you. His love is far more valuable than a paycheck, gold jewelry, or the latest car. He alone grants salvation, gives lasting peace, and brings unshakeable joy. When we truly follow him, we'll have no need to chase anything else.

Lord, I want to serve you, not money. I want to trust you to provide for me, not be enslaved by mammon, amen.

*"Call to me and I will answer you
and tell you great and unsearchable
things you do not know."*

JEREMIAH 33:3

What would you put on a list of "unsearchable things"? That list could get long because, frankly, there is a lot we don't know. We cannot fathom the mind of God.

After all, God knows all these things on our lists of unsearchable things. He knows all things—period. And he invites us to ask him questions when we want to know something.

If you're confounded today, rest in the promise of this verse. God wants to equip you with wisdom and understanding. He longs to help you navigate the relational hardship you're walking through. He wants to give you wisdom as you pursue a new job. He wants to show you how to worship him in a way that brings him glory and you, profound joy.

The almighty creator God, the author and sustainer of life, is available to you. Spend some time today seeking him. Ask him for wisdom and insight. That is a prayer he loves to answer.

*Lord, there's so much I don't yet know. I'm
thankful I can go to you for wisdom and
knowledge when I need them, amen.*

And NOW these THREE remain: FAITH, Hope, & LOVE. 1 Corinthians 13:13

These three remain: faith, hope and love. But the greatest of these is love.

1 CORINTHIANS 13:13

To have faith is to believe that God is big enough to carry out his purposes in your life. To have hope is to believe that no matter what happens, your sovereign God is in complete control. And love is the most precious blessing that humans can both experience and share.

But even if others perceive you as a pillar of faith, if you don't have love, the strength of your faith really doesn't matter. Or if you hope like crazy but do so without loving people, hope has no impact. Love is the premier choice.

Jesus himself taught about the paramount position of love when he identified the two most important commandments: we are to love God and love others.

Look back over your life. When have you loved well? What have you done to demonstrate to God your love for him? In what ways have you sacrificially loved others? How well you love God and how well you love others will determine how much joy you experience on this earth.

Lord—Lord of love—help me to love you and love others today, amen.

My flesh and my heart may fail, but God is the strength of my heart and my portion forever.

PSALM 73:26

The psalmist had intimate knowledge of two things: he would fail, but God would be there. These are two powerful truths.

You may find yourself in a place of failing health. What you used to be able to do, you can no longer do. Whatever your situation, God will be your strength.

You may be discouraged in your current circumstances. Perhaps you are dealing with financial matters or the pressure of difficult decisions. Look again at today's verse and remember that God promised to be your portion: he will prove sufficient for you as he guides, protects, and provides.

No matter where you are today, remember this: God has your heart. He sees your life. He longs to give you hope and peace. Simply ask Him. And wholeheartedly seek Him. Trust that he will supply every ounce of strength you need to face whatever obstacles stand in your way.

Lord, I need to live with as my strength and my portion today. I believe you will provide; help my unbelief, amen.

The grass withers and the flowers fall, but
the word of our God endures forever.

ISAIAH 40:8

*A*s winter becomes spring, we see barren land shoot forth green sprigs that will grow and flower. They may be at their peak in the summer and then wilt and die when autumn arrives.

Isaiah may have had in mind this rhythm of the seasons when he referred to the withering grass and the falling flowers. But that was simply his backdrop for the rock-solid truth that God's Word will never change. That may be especially good news right now if you're walking through a season of lack, or you're bewildered about the mystifying and rapid change swirling all around you. Open the Bible. Look to God's words and find in them help for enduring the chaos and uneasiness. Our eternal God is steady and unchanging, and you can count on that truth even when life feels unsteady.

Despite the change all around you, God is still your rock, the best foundation for life and the true source of wisdom and hope.

Lord, thank you for being sure and unchanging
when I live in the midst of much change, amen.

"The Pharisee stood by himself and prayed: 'God, I thank you that I am not like other people—robbers, evildoers, adulterers— or even like this tax collector.'"

LUKE 18:11

*T*he Pharisee in this story Jesus told didn't get it. He mistakenly thought that Jesus would be impressed with his so-called piety. He was, however, comparing his best characteristics to the worst traits of others. And although he felt he came on top in the comparison, Jesus showed us that he actually lost.

The Pharisee's sin was that of pride, but if he even recognized it in himself, he clearly did not consider it as grievous as robbery, evil-doing, adultery, or deception. And the Pharisee's pride blinded him to his own sin.

Although we human beings continue to be blind to many of our sins, the fact is all of us are sinners. All of us are unworthy recipients of God's outrageous grace. Humility should be the hallmark of our lives, not arrogance. After all, Jesus is the hero of the story, not us. He's the One who rescued mankind.

Lord, thank you for your outrageous grace. Help me live in humility, a beneficiary of so much, amen.

"The kingdom of God is in your midst."

LUKE 17:21

To the Israelites, the kingdom of God meant a piece of land and their sovereign rule in Palestine. It meant a king, like David, ruling from Jerusalem. So when Jesus said these words to the disciples, they must have been confused. Clearly, Jesus wasn't a military man. He wasn't leading a renegade band of revolutionaries to conquer the Romans who now occupied their land.

No, Jesus' kingdom was utterly different from what they had expected. In God's kingdom, the king laid down his life for his people. God's presence with his people—not a plot of land—united them. Hearts are the Lord's temple, indwelled by the Holy Spirit. And this revolution that would overthrow sin, Satan, and death was fueled by love, not fought with swords of metal.

From this side of the cross, we understand more easily and more completely what Jesus meant by these eight words than the disciples ever could. The kingdom of God is not of this world. His kingdom is eternal. And his kingdom will be our eternal home.

Lord, I'm humbled and grateful to be included in your unexpected and eternal kingdom of love. Thank you, amen.

June

"I no longer call you servants....
Instead, I have called you friends."

JOHN 15:15

Talking with the disciples shortly before his death, Jesus uttered the startling words of today's Scripture. Prior to this, people were rarely called a friend of God. Only patriarchs like Moses and Abraham, or kings like David, or prophets like Jeremiah interacted with God as a friend would.

But since the moment he breathed life into Adam, God's desire was to be in relationship with us. Before Adam and Eve sinned, the Father spent time with them, talking and sharing life as they walked through the garden. Sin, however, shattered that friendship. So when Jesus called the disciples his friends, he was ushering in a new way of relating to God.

And you are a beneficiary: you are God's friend. He wants to interact with you about your day. He cares about the things that bother you—and he wants you to be bothered by the things like inequality, poverty, and injustice that bother him. Your friendship with God will bring personal joy as well as a mission: you can represent your Friend's heart in this dying world.

Lord, thank you for the privilege
of being your friend, amen.

June 2

*"His master replied, 'Well done, good
and faithful servant! You have been
faithful with a few things; I will put
you in charge of many things.'"*

MATTHEW 25:23

In the story quoted today, we learn about kingdom math from a story about a man who entrusted his three servants with five bags of gold, two bags, and one. Jesus taught that those who are faithful in very small things will find their responsibilities multiplied. Those who shrink away from doing what God asks may lose all that they have.

The goal of the Christian life should be to be entrusted with more and more responsibility. Thankfully, though, God doesn't give us all this responsibility up front, or we might crumple under the weight. Instead, God steadily increases our capacity to do more. Only when he sees that we'll have good attitudes when we're doing unnoticed things will he entrust us with more to do for him.

Take courage! Know that your heavenly Father sees all the ways you have served him. Trust the training ground he has prepared for you.

*Lord, help me be faithful in small things
so you can entrust me with more—all
and always for your glory, amen.*

*When Christ appears, we shall be like
him, for we shall see him as he is.*

1 JOHN 3:2

Right now we ache to be like Jesus. We are bewildered when we fail—when we sin—but that won't always be the case! When we finally see Jesus face-to-face, we will have been utterly and completely transformed—free from sin, insecurity, worry, and fear.

In the meantime, we choose to have hope. We choose, for instance, to remember that the trials in our lives are temporary, for they will no longer matter on the other side of the grave. The pain we feel and the tears we cry characterize our earthly life. In our eternal home, there will be no more tears. No more weeping. No more worries. Instead we will know a life of God's love as we live in perfect fellowship with Him.

Thankfully, until that time, God graciously allows us glimpses of Jesus, and the light of his presence with us shines brighter during the dark times. Let your glimpses of Jesus remind you that something greater and better is on the heavenly horizon.

*Lord, please help me catch a glimpse
of you today, a glimpse of the
glory that's to come, amen.*

*LORD, the God of Israel, there is no God like you
in heaven above or on earth below—you who
keep your covenant of love with your servants
who continue wholeheartedly in your way.*

1 KINGS 8:23

*I*magine being described as one who lives wholeheartedly for God! You are not divided in your loyalties. You center your life around him and his ways instead of chasing after all the shiny things the world offers. Such wholehearted devotion is a goal worth striving for.

God has already demonstrated this kind of loyal, all-in love to us through his covenant promises. His covenant with Israel was not dependent on the nation's obedience or good works; it was solely based on God's goodness, his steadfastness, his wholehearted love. And, of course, this kind of God always keeps his promises.

God also demonstrated his wholehearted devotion to those he loves when he sent Jesus to die on the cross for our sins. That truth alone can bring hope today. God *wholeheartedly* loves you.

*Lord, thank you for your wholehearted
devotion to me. May I respond with
wholehearted devotion to you, amen.*

"Here I am! I stand at the door and knock. If anyone hears my voice and opens the door, I will come in and eat with that person, and they with me."

REVELATION 3:20

To be with Jesus, we simply need to listen, open, and eat.

First, we must have quiet space in our lives so we can *listen for Jesus' knocking* and actually hear it. We won't open a door if we don't know that someone is there. So we listen and keep alert.

Second, when we hear the knocking of Jesus, we have a choice. We can let him keep knocking, or we can *open the door* to our heart, to our life, and let him in.

Last, we need to spend time with Jesus, the kind of unrushed time that can happen when we *eat a meal* with a friend. Don't ever hesitate to invite him for breakfast, lunch, and dinner.

Choose today to listen, open, and eat.

Lord, keep my ears ready to hear your voice, my hand quick to open the door, and my heart ready to enjoy conversation with you as we linger over a meal, amen.

June 6

*Anyone who does not provide for
their relatives, and especially for their
own household, has denied the faith
and is worse than an unbeliever.*

1 TIMOTHY 5:8

God places us in families for a reason. In the circle of a family, we care for each other when needs arise. We take care of kids, and we share our cars. We help family members who are sick, bringing meals and keeping watch. We shelter those who are struggling. We get on our knees and pray for the wayward ones. We provide for those who cannot pay their bills.

According to Paul, when we don't do these things, our actions deny that we love God. To paraphrase the apostle John, how can we say we love God whom we cannot see but not love family members whom we can? Loving family members is a fulfillment of part of Jesus' two-part commandment to love God and love others.

When we do love others—when we love our family members—our actions show that we are Christ's children. God is glorified when we help those in need.

*Lord, show me specifically what I
can do to tangibly care for someone
in my family today, amen.*

He
HEALS
— the —
broken-
HEARTED
AND
BINDS
— up —
their
WOUNDS.
PSALM
147:3

*He heals the brokenhearted and
binds up their wounds.*

PSALM 147:3

When the psalms were composed, physicians weren't as accessible as they are today. If we get sick, we can get in our cars and drive down the road for help. But if you were injured back then, someone close to you had to care for your wounds. If you were completely heartbroken, you would turn to people nearby for comfort.

Isn't it beautiful that the psalmist describes God as that kind of personal caregiver! He rescues us from the—literally and figuratively speaking—harsh elements of this world, acknowledges our broken heart, and—like the closest family member or friend—takes care of our wounds..

You are the recipient of your heavenly Father's great care. He sees you today. He knows what breaks your heart. He understands why you walk with a limp. He has sent his Spirit to comfort you every moment of every day. He longs to provide you with wound care and ultimately grant you healing. Will you allow him to do so?

*Lord, I give to you my broken heart and
my wounds. Please bring healing, in your
perfect timing and for your glory, amen.*

*I will forgive their wickedness and will
remember their sins no more.*

HEBREWS 8:12

Ours is not an absentminded God who forgets things. What the author of Hebrews was saying is that God allows his love to trump his memory when it comes to our sin. He chooses not to remember our sin because his Son Jesus already paid the ultimate price for it. And so he pardons. He forgives. He chooses to forget because he loves those he is forgiving.

Now God's loving and ready forgiveness when we confess our sins doesn't mean we run around sinning. The complete opposite is true. We instead live with awe and gratitude, for it cost Jesus. We now see it for what it is— evil and awful.

You may be living with shame today. Maybe a particular sin or a series of sins is weighing you down. You may be constantly reminded of your sin because you are living with the consequences daily. Know, however, that you don't need to live under the burden of condemnation because Jesus absolutely set you free once and for all.

*Jesus, thank you for dying for me so my sins
can be forgiven and forgotten, amen.*

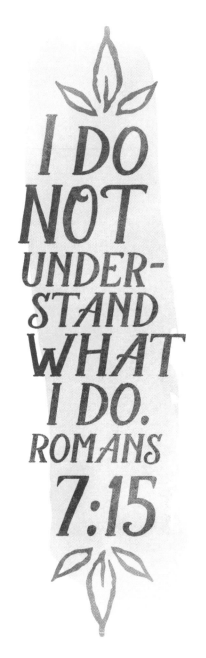

I do not understand what I do. For what I want to do I do not do, but what I hate I do.

ROMANS 7:15

*N*ever do we put "Sin a lot" on our to-do list for the day. But often the very thing we hate to do, we end up doing. Why? You would think we Christ followers would have a handle on this business of sinning. Yet even with the strength of the Holy Spirit within us, we still sin.

Thankfully, there is hope. You can make strides toward walking in the power of the Spirit and escaping the sin cycle. And it involves simply this: talking to God throughout the day, having a continual conversation with him about everything you face, small and large.

Choosing to focus on God by interacting with him about everything might look like this: *Help me love that person who is being rude. Give me strength to endure the next hour. I need help with my attitude. Thank you for providing for me.* This continual conversation invites God into everything you do.

Lord, thank you for the privilege of having an internal monologue with you. May it keep me walking in the Spirit and avoiding sin, amen.

Commit to the LORD whatever you do,
and he will establish your plans.

PROVERBS 16:3

It's not easy to commit our plans to God. We want him to rubberstamp our desires instead of asking if they line up with his desires for us. We have this backward: he commands us to surrender everything to him. When we do, he will "establish [our] plans"

Frustration comes, though, when we quote this verse alone, out of context from the rest of Scripture. After all, sometimes our plans aren't established. What do we do when this verse doesn't seem to apply to our situation? We can choose to acknowledge that we won't always understand our wise God (Isaiah 55:8–9). We can choose to trust in his unfailing love (John 3:16; Romans 8:38–39).

Notice that this verse doesn't guarantee that if we surrender, everything will work out the way we envision it. What this verse does promise is that a life surrendered to God will be characterized by plans that he establishes—and his plans for you are plans for good (Jeremiah 29:11).

Lord, I choose today to surrender afresh and trust you with what I don't understand, amen.

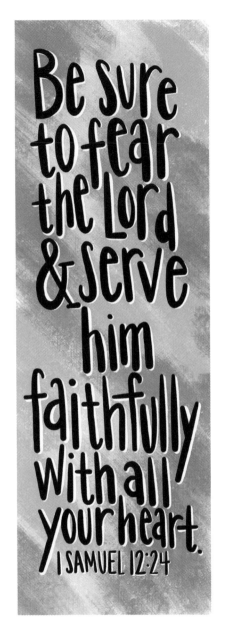

Be sure to fear the LORD and serve him
faithfully with all your heart; consider
what great things he has done for you.

1 SAMUEL 12:24

To fear God and to serve him with our whole heart comes more easily when we remember the amazing things he has done in our lives and especially for our salvation.

Often in the Old Testament, God reminded the Israelites to remember his great deeds and faithfulness. A lot of their rebellion and wandering came because they forgot the goodness of God. Are you forgetting?

Think about the ways God been faithful to you. List some of the "great things" he has done on your behalf. When did he save you? What relationships has he given you that have blessed you? When has God supplied your needs in an unexpected way? In what ways has God helped you in your job? Your finances? Your direction? Your passions? Your ministry?

You have so much to be grateful for. Thank the Lord by serving him "faithfully with all your heart."

Lord, everything I have is a beautiful
gift of love from generous and
gracious you. Thank you, amen.

None of the disciples dared ask him, "Who are you?" They knew it was the Lord.

JOHN 21:12

The Man on the shore had told the tired disciples to cast their nets into the water one more time. The result after they'd come up empty overnight was 153 fish. Then they heard the Man invite them to join him for breakfast, and this is where today's verse comes in. It was no mystery to the disciples who this Man was: the resurrected Jesus, their Friend and their Lord.

Confidence about the claim that Jesus defeated death is crucial because Jesus' resurrection changed everything. It ushered in an eternal spiritual kingdom that cannot be shaken, one established on the foundation of a sinless life, a perfect sacrifice, and a conquering resurrection.

And this resurrected Jesus loves you. He who died for you also rose to life, conquering sin and death! You are a beneficiary of that powerful love. Right now, as you read these words, Jesus is alive, interceding for you, loving you now and for eternity. No wonder they call the gospel the good news!

Lord, thank you for conquering death and ushering in the promise of eternal life with you. I'm grateful, amen.

*"Where were you when I laid
the earth's foundation?"*

JOB 38:4

Job had lost nearly everything—his herds, his crops, his children, and more—and he didn't understand why God would allow him to experience such pain. God, however, explain himself. Instead, he asked Job some questions: "Where were you when?"

Those four words introduced a series of questions in which God listed some of the amazing things he created. Did Job understand what God understood? Did Job have the power God had? These questions silenced Job. Maybe at first glance, God's intense questioning seems cruel, but God was showing that he is bigger than Job, that his understanding, power, and knowledge are greater than Job's . . . and ours.

Our human minds are infinitely smaller than God's. We can't comprehend how the world works, nor can we know how God's plan for our lives will unfold. So we may not fully understand why we're suffering. But one day—and for eternity—we will marvel at the beauty of God's perfect plan.

*Lord, help me trust you and rest
in your plan especially when life is
confusing and painful, amen.*

Restore to me the joy of your salvation and grant me a willing spirit, to sustain me.

PSALM 51:12

This cry comes straight from David's shattered heart. He was utterly broken after the prophet Nathan helped him recognize the magnitude of his sin, of his adultery with Bathsheba and murder of her husband, Uriah. Devastated by the enormity of his sin, David crawled toward the Lord, crying out for mercy and forgiveness.

The beauty of David's life is that he remained a "man after God's heart" despite this tragic foray into sin. He didn't let his actions and their consequences prevent him from running to God. Unfortunately, many of us see our past sin as disqualifying us from receiving God's grace. So we camp in the land of shame.

Whenever you do that, you're believing a lie. God *does* want you back. He *does* love you. He sent his Son to die for you and forgive all your sins. So don't let your sinful choices keep you from returning to God. You will definitely find grace and forgiveness and hope.

Lord, I never want to take my sin lightly, but I also don't want it to keep me away from you, amen.

I no longer live, but Christ lives in me. Galatians 2:20

I have been crucified with Christ and I no longer live, but Christ lives in me.

GALATIANS 2:20

Maybe you've seen a movie that showed Jesus being crucified—getting too close to Calvary makes us awestruck and horrified, uncomfortable yet grateful.

Jesus endured this unspeakable physical pain. Then he endured the unfathomable spiritual pain of being completely forsaken by God, abandoned and alone.

Why? Because he was fulfilling God's call to die for humanity's sins.

So what was Paul talking about here? What does it mean to be crucified with Christ? Simply this: his act of love was so outrageous that it demands a response. And the response is making the deliberate choice to follow after Him.

Being crucified with Christ also means you see sin for what it is: the cause of—the reason for—Jesus' crucifixion. Your own sin becomes a stench to you, so you follow Jesus to the cross to rid yourself of your sin, to find forgiveness, and to be reminded that you can live a new life now—a life of power, hope, and joy.

Lord, I choose today to kneel before the cross in gratitude for your forgiveness and the brand-new life I now can live, amen.

"This is how it will be at the end of the age. The angels will come and separate the wicked from the righteous."

MATTHEW 13:49

Too many of us are shortsighted about life. We only see what's right in front of us—the tasks to complete, relationships to attend to, and bills to pay. But this verse points us to the end and reminds us that there's so much more to life than mowing lawns, meeting quotas, or staying fit. Someday we will reap the reward of a life well lived . . . if we have lived it well.

Knowing there will be an end to our lives, we are wise to ask, "How shall we live?" Are we spending our lives on the right things and in the right places? And what are we doing in our day-to-day life to honor God, to make him smile, to delight him?

Lord, help me live in light of eternity today and tomorrow and every day, amen.

*Every good and perfect gift is from
above, coming down from the Father
of the heavenly lights, who does not
change like shifting shadows.*

JAMES 1:17

God is a good Father who loves to give good gifts to his children. And since he is our wise heavenly Father, he knows what events, experience, character traits, and relationships are best for us. He has the long view in mind.

Even knowing this key truth about God, we can sometimes struggle to see his gifts to us as good. We experience an unexpected and tragic loss, and we don't understand why. Or we wonder if God is truly good when things go wrong.

James reminded us that God is the source of all good gifts. But at the beginning of the chapter, he had encouraged us to consider trials that come our way as a reason for pure joy because they will strengthen our faith. So whether God's gifts come in the form of trials or in the form of answered prayers, remember that God is good in both circumstances. He is always good.

*Lord, keep me aware of the gifts you
graciously and generously give me.
I want to be grateful, amen.*

June 18

*You know we never used flattery,
nor did we put on a mask to cover
up greed—God is our witness.*

1 THESSALONIANS 2:5

*M*any people struggle with the church because of the issue of money. Based on various experiences, some people perceive that churches are all about separating you from your paycheck.

Take note, though, of what Paul said here. First, he and his fellow workers didn't flatter people in order to compel them to donate to a cause or meet a need. And when talking about the church's financial needs, Paul also didn't say one thing and mean another. He was authentic in his concern for the church; his motive was never greed.

Serving God is impossible when we serve money. Jesus made this clear. So Paul made sure his ministry was above reproach. How about you? Are you handling the money God has entrusted to you in a way that pleases and honors him? Are you generous? Do you see money as a tool or something to grab onto? How wonderful that Paul is an example of how to view and deal with money.

*Lord, I want to be free from greed. I want
to be free to be generous, amen.*

IT IS THE *Lord* YOUR GOD YOU MUST *Follow,* AND HIM YOU MUST *Revere.*

DEUTERONOMY 13:4

It is the Lord your God you must follow, and him you must revere. Keep his commands and obey him; serve him and hold fast to him.

DEUTERONOMY 13:4

It used to be easier to go to the grocery store and pick up some ice cream. The options were fairly limited: chocolate, vanilla, strawberry, or chocolate chip. Today more choices exist, including low-fat, lactose-free, designer flavors, seasonal varieties, the knock-off brand, and the name brand that is on sale. *Someone just tell me what to buy!*

When we choose how to live, we also have options: whom will we follow? The world has its suggestions (money, possessions, status). We can pour ourselves into our family or home. The Hindus, Muslims, Buddhists, and others offer spiritual paths. *Someone just tell me whom to follow!*

God's Word does exactly that. Speaking on behalf of the Almighty, Moses clearly said, "It is the Lord your God you must follow, and him you must revere." Doing so will be challenging at times, but you can know you are definitely on the right path.

Lord, thank you for taking the guesswork out of whom to follow and invest my life in. Help me follow you closely and honor you all my days.

*Let us therefore make every effort to do what
leads to peace and to mutual edification.*

ROMANS 14:19

We live in a divided world—divided by
opinions, economics, race, religion,
politics, and more. There doesn't seem to be
room for healthy discussion or kind disagree-
ment. Issues seem reduced to "You're for me
or against me," with very little in between.

Paul encouraged believers here to make
every effort to be peacemakers who are deeply
concerned about the feelings and thoughts
of others. This is a diplomatic call—a wooing
toward kindness and compassion in the way
we interact with people who differ from us.

Remember, the person holding the opinion
is still just a person who longs to be understood, validated, and loved. That person is
more than his or her opinion. When you serve
as a peacemaker—and all of us are to do so—
listen with a desire to understand rather than
be understood. Choose to be like Jesus.

*Lord, I want to treat people as people, not as
opinions. Use me as a peacemaker today, amen.*

FAITH WITHOUT DEEDS IS DEAD. JAMES 2:26

As the body without the spirit is dead,
so faith without deeds is dead.

JAMES 2:26

The moment you see or touch the body of a person who has died, you know he or she is not there. That person's spirit has departed.

James used this universal fact of death in an analogy to cement the important truth that faith without actions is the same as a dead body. It is only an empty shell of faith.

But the opposite is also true. Once we've been saved, that reality should inform our entire lives. After all, our heart is no longer the same. It used to be dead in sin, but the Holy Spirit has given it new life.

May the outcome of this rebirth be our faith in action. May we—because of the presence of the Holy Spirit within us—find that we can't help but love the unlovely, feed the poor, pray for the sick, and forgive our enemies. What a witness to the world of a living faith in Jesus!

Lord, I want my faith to be alive, pointing
people to you who have forgiven my
sins and changed my heart, amen.

*"I will redeem you with an outstretched
arm and with mighty acts of judgment."*

EXODUS 6:6

God spoke these words to Moses before he went to Pharaoh, reminding Moses that he would be with him in everything. Yet Moses argued with God because, at this point, the Israelites were tired of hearing Moses talk about God delivering Israel. Moses said, "My own people won't listen to me anymore. How can I expect Pharaoh to listen? I'm such a clumsy speaker!"

God tried to reassure reluctant Moses through miraculous signs and wonders. God did not call Moses to go before Pharaoh without giving him words, a plan, and power.

Maybe God has encouraged you to do something that seems impossible. And perhaps you've been like Moses, ready with very logical excuses as to why it wouldn't possibly work.

You'll miss the miracles unless you take that first step. So say those words you're afraid to say. Take that leap of faith that scares you to death. In those moments you feel helpless and frightened, you will see how faithful and powerful God is.

*Lord, give me courage to take steps of faith
so I don't miss your miracles. Amen.*

"Blessed are the poor in spirit, for theirs is the kingdom of heaven."

MATTHEW 5:3

The word *kingdom* brings to mind silk and satin; feasts and wine; wealthy and influential people. But Jesus described a completely different kind of kingdom here. It's an upside-down one where the rich are (spiritually) poor, the (spiritually) poor are welcomed into the kingdom, and the meek inherit everything. What a beautiful reversal our Lord accomplished for all of us. Yes, including you.

Have you ever felt small or unworthy? Welcome to the kingdom. Have you battled money woes? Welcome to the kingdom. Do you feel "less than"? Have you noticed all the "perfect people" out there and felt unqualified to follow Jesus? Again, welcome to the kingdom.

Hurting and broken folks have no trouble entering Jesus' realm because they clearly recognize their great need for him. So, welcome to the kingdom, you beautiful saint! You are loved—and always will be. You may feel poor in spirit, but you are rich in God's kingdom.

Lord, thank you for showing me that I need you and for welcoming me to your kingdom, amen.

*Be like-minded, be sympathetic, love one
another, be compassionate and humble.*

1 PETER 3:8

*L*ike-mindedness, sympathy, love, compassion, and humility—the apostle Peter
called first-century believers to demonstrate
these traits in their life together.

To be like-minded means to share similar
passions and goals, get along, and joyfully pursue ministry together.

To have sympathy is to see things so clearly
from another's perspective that you share his
or her feelings.

To love is to act according to the truth that
all people are different, but they all deserve to
be accepted.

To have compassion is to be moved to
action on behalf of someone who is suffering.

To have humility is to consider others
as more important than yourself. It's also to
choose to humble yourself under God.

Not only do all these traits make for a great
church community, but they can also enrich
the community of a family. Consider today how
you might bring like-mindedness, sympathy,
love, compassion, and humility into your home.

*Lord, thank you for enabling us to do in
our church and our homes what you call
us to do—to be like-minded, amen.*

Above all else, guard your heart, for everything you do flows from it.

PROVERBS 4:23

Have you ever said something and wondered where that comment came from? Or maybe an idea crossed your mind that you wouldn't tell your best friend about—and exactly where did that come from? Or maybe you did something completely out of character and ask yourself, *What was I thinking?*

We read in Proverbs that everything—our words, our thoughts, our choices, our decisions, our priorities—comes from our hearts. When a heart is full of God's love, beautiful words and ideas flow from it. Are you paying attention to your heart?

The wise writer of Proverbs warned us to guard our hearts. We need to protect our hearts against bitterness, impatience, and greed, against jealousy, idolatry, and anger. These traits will overtake our hearts if we let them. We must also guard our hearts against unsafe people, unhealthy relationships, and ungodly activities and entertainment.

Protect your heart so that beautiful words, ideas, and actions flow from it, for your good and God's glory!

Lord, please show me where I need to protect my heart, amen.

*I know what it is to be in need, and I know what
it is to have plenty. I have learned the secret
of being content in any and every situation.*

PHILIPPIANS 4:12

It is definitely not natural for us human beings to be content. Yet Paul learned the secret of being content and lived it out "in any and every situation," whether he was needy or needed nothing, whether he was hungry or well fed.

The secret is trusting God. Trusting in his sovereignty over our lives. Trusting in his good and loving and, yes, mysterious ways. Paul said: "I can do all this [be content whatever the circumstances] through him who gives me strength" (v. 13). The secret to contentment is looking to God for strength to endure. At times Paul had all he needed, and at other times he suffered with needs. And in either case, he chose contentment. Whether it's a job loss, a cancer diagnosis, a tough marriage, a wayward child, or any of a number of things, we are able to be content when we look to God.

*Lord, help me keep my eyes on you, who
loves me and has good plans for me, amen.*

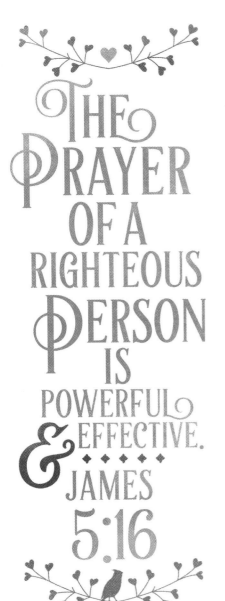

THE PRAYER OF A RIGHTEOUS PERSON IS POWERFUL & EFFECTIVE. JAMES 5:16

The prayer of a righteous person
is powerful and effective.

JAMES 5:16

What is your reaction when you read that verse? Do you feel intimidated? We may not think this verse describes us because of that scary word *righteous*. We are well aware of our sins; seldom do we feel righteous. So we disqualify ourselves from the hope of this statement.

But this verse absolutely does apply to you, for Jesus has made you righteous. Because of his life, death, and resurrection, you are placed in right standing with God. Your position as his child is utterly secure because it's based on Jesus' righteousness.

With this spiritual truth in mind, you can kneel before God knowing that your prayers will be powerful and effective. You can pray that God would supply your needs and be assured that provision will come in surprising ways.

You have been made righteous: Jesus took on your sins and died on the cross so that you could be dressed in his righteousness. God hears your prayers and answers. Rejoice in that amazing truth today.

Lord, thank you that I'm made righteous by you,
and thank you that you hear my prayers, amen.

*One thing I ask from the Lord, this only
do I seek: that I may dwell in the house
of the Lord all the days of my life.*

PSALM 27:4

The house of the Lord represents God's presence with his people. God's house was first the portable tabernacle of Moses' day and then, during Solomon's reign, the glorious temple of God. Inside the temple was the Holy of Holies, and there God's presence rested.

The psalmist, David, could imagine nothing more wonderful than being in the house where the Lord himself dwelled. That was, in fact, his only desire: he sought after nothing except being in God's glorious presence.

Thanks to Jesus' death on the cross, we can do what David sang about. Forgiven of our sin, we can enter into the presence of our holy God. We also have been blessed with the indwelling of God's Holy Spirit. Therefore, God is present with you—within you—all the time. What an astounding, surprising, eternal-life-altering truth!

*Lord, may I recognize your presence with
me every moment of every day. May I hear
your voice and—out of loving gratitude for
your death on my behalf—obey, amen.*

*Be on your guard; stand firm in the
faith; be courageous; be strong.*

1 CORINTHIANS 16:13

Life is not meant to be lived lacka-
daisically. We are not to be passive
Christians, allowing evil to take hold, morals
to crumble, and the helpless to suffer as we
sink comfortably into our couches. Instead,
Paul called believers to be alert, courageous,
and strong—words that imply vigilance and
action!

But how do we live with alertness? How
can we "stand firm in the faith; be courageous;
[and] be strong"? The truth is, we can't. Left
to ourselves to live the Christian life, we will
only fail.

Thankfully, we are not left to ourselves,
and there is hope. When you asked Jesus to
be the Lord of your life, he sent the Holy Spirit
to live within you. Therein lies our hope: the
Spirit empowers us to be "on our guard," to be
brave, and to live courageously. What a gift!

*Lord, thank you for the gift of your Holy Spirit
in my life—and, Spirit, empower me to be
a gutsy and active Christian who makes a
difference for the Lord in this world! Amen.*

"I will pour out my Spirit on all people.
Your sons and daughters will prophesy,
your old men will dream dreams,
your young men will see visions."

JOEL 2:28

Joel's prophecy points to Pentecost, the birthday of the church in Acts 2 when the Holy Spirit of God was poured out on the believers. With this appearance of the Holy Spirit, the disciples spoke in other tongues and, later, would prophesy and see visions of God.

The apostle Paul, for instance, met Jesus when he was traveling to Damascus to arrest and kill followers of Jesus. Paul's vision of the resurrected Lord transformed Paul from murderer of Christians to Christian teacher, pastor, and apologist.

Isn't it amazing that the same Spirit who raised Jesus from the dead and who turned the ancient world upside down through these first-century Christians is the same Spirit who resides in you right now? What beautiful potential we all have to impact the world for our God.

Lord, thank you for the Holy Spirit. Please
use me—empowered by him—to make a
difference in this world for you, amen.

July

I WILL FORGIVE THEIR WICKEDNESS & WILL REMEMBER THEIR SINS NO MORE. JEREMIAH 31:34

"I will forgive their wickedness and will remember their sins no more."

JEREMIAH 31:34

*H*ave you ever had a friend who knows something bad that you did and never lets you forget it? Thankfully, God is not at all like that "friend." We find evidence in today's verse where he promised the nation of Israel something beautiful: a clean slate.

God promised to forgive their wickedness. He resolved to not remember their sins.

This beautiful promise foreshadowed what he would do—and does do—for all of us in the crucifixion. This promise is for you today. God will forgive your sins. He will not remember them or hold them against you.

In light of that, God commands you and me to forgive people who have sinned against us—and the Holy Spirit enables us to do just that. You can forgive. You can choose to stop thinking about their sins against you. You can reflect the amazing love of Jesus in the way you treat those who have sinned against you.

Lord, thank you for not remembering my sins. Help me honor you by forgiving those who have hurt me, amen.

July 2

*LORD, the God of Israel, there is no God like
you in heaven or on earth—you who keep
your covenant of love with your servants
who continue wholeheartedly in your way.*

2 CHRONICLES 6:14

*G*od always keeps his promises. The God of
truth could not do otherwise!

God spells out his promises in what is
called a covenant, and he cannot by his very
nature break it. The covenants he makes are
based on his unchanging love. May we love
him wholeheartedly in return.

To love God this way means to do so
single-mindedly: we don't chase after things
we might make into idols. Instead of being
devoted to success or a perfect life, we are
devoted to serving God and glorifying him.

When we live wholeheartedly for him, we
come to know him more completely. We begin
to appreciate even more that he is faithful,
strong, capable, holy, grace-filled, intelligent,
and beautiful. He relentlessly pursues his
people, like a good shepherd searches for a lost
sheep. That's what God's covenant love does.

May you both rest and rejoice in God's
sacrificial, pursuing love today.

*Lord, I'm grateful for the promises you make
and keep. I'm grateful for your love, amen.*

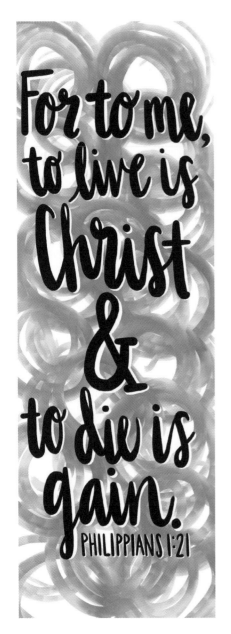

For to me, to live is Christ and to die is gain.

PHILIPPIANS 1:21

*N*ote the irony. The apostle Paul—who wrote the letter to the Philippians from prison—had once tried to put Christians behind bars. Paul had come to realize, though, that his time in prison was actually fruitful for ministry: he shared Christ with all his guards, and he had a great deal of freedom to write on behalf of the gospel.

Paul knew that if he continued to live, this fruitful prison ministry would flourish. But he loved Jesus Christ with his whole heart. And Paul's love for Jesus superseded even his passion for his work on Jesus' behalf!

Do you realize that Philippians 1:21 applies to you as well? As long as you live in this world, you will be able to live for Jesus Christ, serve his people, and share his love. But when you die, you will experience great gain as you live in the presence of Jesus, your Savior.

You can say with Paul, "To live is Christ and to die is gain."

Lord, I want to live wholly for you today—and I thank you that I will one day see you face-to-face, amen.

Fear God and keep his commandments,
for this is the duty of all mankind.

ECCLESIASTES 12:13

*A*t first glance, this imperative sounds harsh. *Fear. Commandments. Duty.* But remember, God's commandments aren't the same as a drill instructor making us do extreme things to prove our total obedience.

God's heart for us is evident throughout his commandments. They are guidelines established for our welfare, instituted because he loves us. We don't steal because stealing impoverishes our hearts and harms someone God loves. We don't murder because it takes the life of one of his children. We honor our parents because God has placed us in their family, and the family is the foundation of a healthy, moral society.

Fearing God means we follow him with more passion than we follow after the things of this world. We value God's opinion of us more than we value the opinions of others.

Living this way—living according to God's commandments—will bring not only a sense of wholeness as you live the way your Creator designed you to live but also deeper joy.

Lord, I want to honor you by keeping
your commandments today and
every day. Please help me, amen.

*"Where your treasure is, there
your heart will be also."*

MATTHEW 6:21

In the Sermon on the Mount, Jesus told about a man who found a treasure and then sold everything he owned to buy the field where the treasure was buried.

Treasure is what you value most. Treasure is often beautiful and always costly. And many things vie for that status in our hearts and our lives. What do you treasure?

We can chase the wrong treasure in this life. That happens when we wrongly believe that this life is all we have, so we grab everything we can. We go after treasures like fame, money, position, and power. If we live for those earthly treasures, we will never know better and eternal treasure.

Jesus called us to "store up for yourselves treasures in heaven" (v. 20). What does that look like? When we speak and act with love, compassion, gospel truth, kindness, peace, and joy, we are storing up treasures in heaven. We are investing in treasures of eternal value, not the world's treasures that will turn to dust.

*Lord, please teach me more about what it looks
like to store up my treasure in heaven, amen.*

*"If the world hates you, keep in
mind that it hated me first."*

JOHN 15:18

When we are walking in obedience to Jesus, we must expect pushback. When we love others with abandon, give with generosity, and tell the truth without hesitation, we will encounter hate in various forms. Here, Jesus reminded his disciples that he had been hated. Because he was hated, we can find help from him when we are hated. Jesus knows what it's like. He empathizes.

Not only that, but when we suffer for doing what is right, when we are persecuted because of our commitment to the gospel, we are sharing in Jesus' sufferings "in order that we may also share in his glory" (see Romans 8:17). Persecution and hatred may therefore mean that we're shining God's light in the darkness of this world.

Whenever you're experiencing this kind of hate, learn the art of rejoicing despite it. The hate may be confirming that the Lord is obviously alive in you!

Oh, Jesus well understands your situation. He will comfort you and enable you to endure.

*Lord, I don't like to be hated. It hurts. Empower
me to love even when I am hated, amen.*

*The angel of the LORD encamps around
those who fear him, and he delivers them.*

PSALM 34:7

Whatever your theory about who the angel of the Lord is (some say Jesus; others say a powerful messenger sent by God; others say God the Father appearing briefly in human form), the truth remains that this angel protects those who fear God. And, according to this verse, the angel also delivers God-fearers from whatever holds them captive.

What a beautiful picture for us! When we fear God—when we revere, worship, and submit to him—he promises to be near us, to be right where we live. Whatever problems we may face, he has promised deliverance.

What are you facing today? Whatever you face right now, you have the privilege of laying all these worries and burdens at God's feet.

God promises to be near you and to walk with you through the trials. And in his perfect timing, he will bring the deliverance you need.

*Lord, help me be aware that you are
near me. Help me trust that you're in
the process of delivering me, amen.*

The day of the Lord will come
like a thief in the night.

1 THESSALONIANS 5:2

The Day of the Lord is referred to throughout the Old and New Testaments, and it refers to the ultimate day of reckoning when God's justice will finally prevail. All wrongs will be made right.

But it won't come on a specified day. Just like the day of your death, you won't know when the Day of the Lord will occur. So be ready.

To be living with an awareness of the Day of the Lord means to live as if it will arrive any moment. It means being faithful to God, trusting him, and choosing to follow him no matter what temptations come your way.

Furthermore, we want to be faithful stewards of all God has given us, so that when he returns, he will find us living in a way that honors him, waiting expectantly, and serving him with joy.

What a blessing it will be when God finds you faithful!

Lord, I want to be faithful to you every
day, no matter the circumstances or the
pressure. So please help me live each day
in light of eternity with you, amen.

"Ask and it will be given to you; seek and you will find; knock and the door will be opened to you."

LUKE 11:9

*C*onsider the exciting implications of what Jesus said here: if you have needs, ask your generous Father to meet those needs, and he will grant your request. God will answer, but sometimes, his answers don't make sense to us, or we grow tired of waiting for him to answer. We come to the conclusion that God is either deaf to our cries, or he simply has better things to do than to grant our requests.

Prayer is more than asking for stuff, though. It's spending time with God. And as you spend time with him, you'll begin to develop his heart for others. Suddenly you'll find that you're not asking for a list of things you want, but you're asking that his will would be done just as it is in heaven. And his will could mean his saying no to a request you have.

Trust that God knows exactly what's best for you. Choose to trust his answers to your prayers.

Lord, I want what you want for me. Please have your way in my life, amen.

*Jesus was indignant. He reached out
his hand and touched the man. "I
am willing," he said. "Be clean!"*

MARK 1:41

Jesus said these words to a man with
leprosy who had dropped to his knees
and begged, "If you are willing, you can make
me clean" (v. 40). And Jesus didn't react with
anger to the leper's request. Instead, Jesus
was most likely saddened by the leprosy that
plagued him and perhaps moved by the leper's words that implied he didn't feel worthy of
Jesus' attention. So Jesus touched the leper.

Consider for a moment how radical that is.
Jesus touched an untouchable, a man whose
disease had long isolated him from community.
According to Jewish law, Jesus would become
unclean if he chose to touch the sick man.

Jesus didn't care about that. His concern
for the leper superseded his concern about
ritual cleanness. Love overcame law.

And when Jesus touched the unclean
man, the man was immediately clean.

Take heart from this scene in Jesus' life.
You may feel untouchable some days, but
Jesus actively pursues you, touches you, and
heals you. That is good news!

*Lord, I'm grateful that you are willing to touch
me and make me clean today! Amen to that!*

LIFE does not CONSIST in an ABUNDANCE of possessions.

LUKE 12:15

"Watch out! Be on your guard against all kinds of greed; life does not consist in an abundance of possessions."

LUKE 12:15

Greed does not help us accomplish the goals of God's kingdom. Why? Because at its core, greed is about self and satisfying that self. Furthermore, greed for financial bliss keeps us from following God: we can't serve both God and money.

And, as you've heard it said, we can't take with us whatever we find ourselves being greedy for. Yet the world's deceitful and alluring voice ignores that fact. And Satan knows that if he can get believers chasing wealth no matter the cost, they will have little positive effect—if any—on God's kingdom. If Satan convinces us that we'll be happy only when we reach a certain income level, he'll keep us on his treadmill longer and longer.

If greed is lurking in your heart, here's the simple—but not especially easy—antidote: joyful giving. Let go of the wealth you've chased. Happily give it away, and you'll break greed's hold on you.

Lord, thank you for the mirror of your Word, and please free me from greed, amen.

*"Go and make disciples of all nations,
baptizing them in the name of the Father
and of the Son and of the Holy Spirit."*

MATTHEW 28:19

*T*he resurrected Jesus uttered this holy mandate before he ascended into heaven. He longed for the disciples to take what they had learned about Jesus and share it with the world.

Jesus longs for us to do the same today. We have experienced Jesus and experienced life change. Instead of reveling in that transformation, we are—like the disciples—to share it in the world.

Jesus didn't ask his disciples to start programs. He didn't encourage them to build buildings. Instead, he gave them a mandate based on what they knew and had experienced. Jesus commanded them to tell people about forgiveness of sins and living with him as Lord, just as he had.

No matter where you find yourself in life today, you have the same opportunity to carry out the Great Commission. Pray that God would show you whom to disciple and then do so with prayer and joy.

Lord, your mandate is straightforward: love people one at a time and share what I've learned about you. Please help me, amen.

The LORD your GOD goes with you; He will never leave you nor forsake you. Deuteronomy 31:6

Be strong and courageous. Do not be afraid or terrified because of them, for the LORD your God goes with you; he will never leave you nor forsake you.

DEUTERONOMY 31:6

*T*he opposite of *strong and courageous* is *weak and fearful*, traits that Moses alluded to in the second part of today's verse. Much in our lives can make us tremble in fear. The economy. Difficult people. Our jobs. The state of our families. But God's Word reminds us that we don't have to be held hostage by our fears. Instead, we can turn to him, ask him to give us his strength, and then live full of courage and grit.

Also fueling this courage and grit is the amazing truth that God promises to never, ever leave us. He will not forsake us; he will not turn his back on us. No, he is constant. He walks with us today, and he will walk with us all our tomorrows.

Lord, I am so humbled and strengthened by your promise to stay with me and to never turn your back on me. Help me live mindful of that today and every day, amen.

 July 14

Children are a heritage from the LORD,
offspring a reward from him.

PSALM 127:3

What a beautiful gift children are! Maybe you have children, or maybe you're connected to children through your extended family, friends, church, work, or neighborhood. Wherever we come in contact with children, it's important to see them as Jesus did—valuable, worthy of his love and attention, and uniquely receptive to the kingdom of God.

Children teach us to have simple faith. They trust and believe the truths of the kingdom more readily than our cynical minds do. They believe big.

Children model dependence. They can't do everything adults can do, so they have to humbly rely on other people for pretty much everything. They serve as an example of trust that food, clothes, shelter, and love will come.

Children tend to love well—even difficult people. Their innocent, generous affection encourages us to approach our relationships this way.

Children truly are a reward and a blessing!

Lord, thank you for placing children in my life.
Help me to learn from them today, amen.

Be completely humble and gentle; be
patient, bearing with one another in love.

EPHESIANS 4:2

When we encounter a frustrating person, our first response is typically irritation or anger. We want to criticize and point out flaws. Or we want to establish that we are right so someone else can be the bad guy and we'll feel better about ourselves. When interactions with people get stressful, we find it hard to be patient.

And our fallback is pride, arrogance, and impatience. But Paul reminded us that, as believers, we must operate differently. We must live out kingdom values. To be specific, Paul encouraged us to be completely humble and gentle. Not partially, but completely. And not by gritting our teeth because we're supposed to be kind, but to be wholeheartedly extending Christlike kindness. We are to have a servant's heart of love like our Savior has.

Think about a frustrating person in your life. Maybe someone who knows exactly how to annoy you. Ask the Holy Spirit to work in your heart so you can be humble, gentle, and patient, extending genuine Christlike love.

Lord, I need you to help me love this
difficult person. Please help me, amen.

"I AM WHO I AM."

EXODUS 3:14

*I*magine hearing God speak these five words, declaring his power and might and majesty. As Yahweh, he exists eternally and can therefore easily come to our aid when we are feeling weak and helpless.

Consider, for instance, what God did to deliver the Israelites from an impossible situation. Pharaoh pursued them on one side with a mighty army of chariots. On the other side was a vast sea. And yet, God, the great I Am, did the impossible: he created a pathway through the sea, and his people crossed on dry land.

Later in Israel's history, God also made the mighty walls of Jericho quake and fall to rubble. He opened the womb of a virgin and brought forth his Son. And he raised that Son from the dead so we could walk through our own Red Sea of death to God himself. The gap between our holy God and us unholy human beings seemed unbridgeable, but Jesus made himself the bridge for us.

Lord, you are the Great I Am, and you love me. I know you will take care of me today, and I thank you, amen.

*Those parts of the body that seem
to be weaker are indispensable.*

1 CORINTHIANS 12:22

Whenever you stub a toe—a seemingly unimportant appendage—you will better understand this verse. That toe is not a heart or a lung: it doesn't sustain the body. It's not a liver, cleaning our system of toxins. It's not a protective immune system or nerve system, but that toe is necessary: it helps us walk and balance. And when it's throbbing, we absolutely remember its importance.

As Paul pointed out, this principle applies to the body of Christ. We too often honor most those people who have up-front, flashy gifts. When this behavior discourages fellow believers—those with behind-the-scenes roles—the body of believers is weakened. Every single part of a body is important, every single part of Christ's body serves a specific and vital role, and every single part of Christ's body needs to be appreciated and affirmed.

Are you feeling like a toe on the body of Christ today? Remember this: you play an important role.

*Lord, help me be aware of who in the
body of Christ needs to be encouraged
with words of love and appreciation—and
then prompt me to speak them, amen.*

The heart is deceitful above all things and beyond cure. Who can understand it?

JEREMIAH 17:9

It's not exactly a beautiful devotional thought that our hearts are wicked and beyond repair. But consider Jeremiah's question: "Who can understand it?" The answer is God, and that is a beautiful thought. God understands the broken and wicked heart, and he has from the beginning of man's waywardness back in the garden of Eden. Adam and Eve knew they had sinned. Little did they know that their choice to follow their wishes rather than God's command would usher in an age of wickedness and sin.

Yet God had a plan for dealing with the wicked heart of mankind and, at the same time, restoring humanity's relationship with him. God sent his Son to earth to carry to the cross every deceitful heart.

Without Jesus' death and resurrection we are beyond cure. But hallelujah! He is risen! There is a cure for our deceitful hearts.

Lord, I'm grateful that you chose to remedy my sinful and wandering heart. Please help me walk with you in gratitude and with a heart you have changed, amen.

*"Come, buy . . . without money
and without cost."*

ISAIAH 55:1

Imagine walking into a gourmet grocery store and lingering over the dark chocolate delicacies, the exotic fruit, and the imported cheese. As you look around, a clerk comes up to you and hands you a card. It reads: "Fill your cart for free today." What joy you'd have walking the aisles, finding special treats, and putting them into your cart.

Now, wouldn't you be grateful and excited about this amazing opportunity? You would probably tell everyone you know!

Think for a minute about the salvation Jesus offers. He gave himself freely in death on the cross so we could freely receive such priceless gifts as love, hope, and eternal life. Aren't you grateful and excited about this amazing opportunity? Doesn't it make sense to tell everyone you know! Think about those people in your life who would benefit from hearing about this generous God. Spend some time praying for each one, asking God to give you excited words about his free salvation.

*Lord, thank you for your gift of salvation: while
it is free to me, I know it cost you everything.
May I live a life of gratitude, amen.*

July 20

He knows the way that I take; when he has tested me, I will come forth as gold.

JOB 23:10

A refinery is a place that heats metal so hot that it becomes liquid, and the impurities rise to the top, where they are removed. When the refining process is finished and the metal has cooled, the raw lump of gold—recently full of dirt and other impurities—is now shiny and pure. And in that state the metal is both useful and valuable.

Think of the fiery trials you walk through as one way God refines your character and strengthens your faith. You may be tempted to try to run out of those fires, recuperating instead of walking through them.

But don't! This verse promises that not only does God know the pathway through the fire that you're walking, but he will use that journey to refine you. You'll be a different person when you emerge from the flames, and that is cause for rejoicing.

Lord, as I face this fiery trial, give me your perspective that this refinement is for my good and your glory. Bring me forth as gold, I pray, amen.

Though one may be overpowered,
two can defend themselves. A cord of
three strands is not quickly broken.

ECCLESIASTES 4:12

There is power in community, and there is weakness in isolation.

Yet we forget that when someone has hurt us deeply. When that happens, our tendency is to withdraw and lick our wounds. The last thing we want to do is to jump back into community.

But the author of Ecclesiastes clearly showed us one reason why life is best lived with others: good relationships protect us and strengthen us—especially when that third strand is the Lord himself.

Still, you may be reluctant to join in with others. You may prefer a more private life. But the truth is, when Jesus saved us, he placed us in his body of believers for good reason. One reason is this paradoxical truth: what wounds is what heals. If you've been wounded in community, the pathway to wholeness is healthy, godly community.

The choice is yours. Protection and strength await you in a community of fellow believers. Will you take a baby step toward one?

Lord, give me the courage I need to enter
into a community of your people, amen.

We do not lose heart. Though outwardly
we are wasting away, yet inwardly we
are being renewed day by day.

2 CORINTHIANS 4:16

One hundred percent of us are growing older, are—to use Paul's words—"wasting away." And we see such decay all around us: bread goes moldy, fences wear out and fall down, and our dog starts having difficulty standing up. Paul overshadowed this sad news with quite a surprising and amazing truth.

Paul said, yes, decay is happening. Yes, we are wasting away. But then came the word *yet.* Yet God is renewing us. As we grow older, our souls can grow more beautiful and wiser every single day.

But this renewal of our soul happens only when we are open to God's transformative work. After we die, our bodies will be renewed, but now, even on this decaying earth, God can and will renew our souls, using "our light and momentary troubles" to refine us and achieve for us eternal glory (v. 17).

Lord, thank you for the hope of this
inward renewal. I welcome your
promised transformation of me,
from the inside out, amen.

*The wages of sin is death, but the gift of God
is eternal life in Christ Jesus our Lord.*

ROMANS 6:23

*N*o one likes death. This Scripture reminds us that the outcome of a sin-filled life is just that. We "earn" death because of our sinful nature.

This, on the surface, seems like terrible news. Born into sin, we can't help but live for ourselves, chase after number one (us!), and do things that hurt us, others, and God.

Thankfully, the word *but* stands in the middle of this verse. Yes, it's true that we are sinners, doomed to die. *But* God has resolved the terrible dilemma by sending Jesus Christ. Sinless, Jesus took our place on the cross we deserved so that we can escape death and instead enjoy eternal life with him.

This is a gift. We don't deserve it; we haven't earned it.

But because of God's outrageous generosity, you can relax today knowing that your life eternal is secure in his capable hands. Death doesn't have a grip on you; life does.

*Lord, I am awed by and grateful for your
generous grace toward me. Thank you
for sending Jesus to die for my sins, for
delivering me from death to life, amen.*

*What is more, I consider everything a
loss because of the surpassing worth of
knowing Christ Jesus my Lord, for whose
sake I have lost all things. I consider
them garbage, that I may gain Christ.*

PHILIPPIANS 3:8

Why was Paul talking about garbage? Because he wanted to make an important point. He was saying here that everything he'd had prior to Christ—his prestige, his fame within his religious sphere, his theological knowledge, his political influence, his respected status as a Roman citizen—meant nothing to him in comparison to knowing Jesus Christ.

When we don't keep a keen focus on Jesus, we may begin to value the garbage more than we value the Savior. When we forget that Jesus is the greatest treasure we can pursue and we instead pursue things, wealth, power, prestige, and fame, we do so at the expense of our soul. The only One who will truly fulfill us is Jesus Christ.

May you live with Jesus as your most treasured relationship. May you revel in him, not in stuff or acclaim, and therefore be deeply satisfied and content.

*Lord, you are my treasure. Help me recognize
when I'm chasing garbage instead of you, amen.*

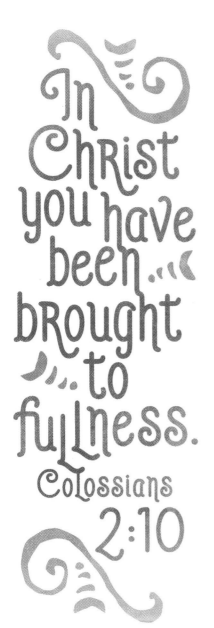

In Christ you have been... brought ...to fullness. Colossians 2:10

*In Christ all the fullness of the Deity
lives in bodily form, and in Christ you
have been brought to fullness. He is the
head over every power and authority.*

COLOSSIANS 2:9–10

God is fully in Christ, and Christ is fully in you. What an amazing truth!

Yet you may not feel like you're complete; you may feel that you're lacking in something important. But the reality is, because of Jesus, you have been made full. He has filled you up with himself.

Still, at times you feel empty. What enables you to move through life as you struggle with depression or anxiety or overwhelming fear? Try gently reminding yourself of the truth that the God of the universe is for you, not against you. That he sent his Son to die for you, so you could have fullness of life. That his love for you is not dependent on you, but is dependent on his faithfulness to his nature. God is love.

The God who is above every power and authority has chosen to love you. Remind yourself of this foundational, purpose-giving truth.

*Lord, please help me remind myself of your love,
the fullness of your love that fills me, amen.*

Start children off on the way they should go, and even when they are old they will not turn from it.

PROVERBS 22:6

When we read the Proverbs, we need to remember that they are meant to be general instructions for life; they are not to be regarded as solid guarantees.

Yes, of course parents are supposed to do everything they can to train their children to know God. This training comes through words and through actions. But, we must remember, children are human beings with free will and sinful hearts who therefore are prone to wander from God's ways.

Parents' responsibility is to train themselves out of their parenting job—but they are to continue to pray like crazy once their children are launched. Even if your children stray, remember that God loves them more than you do and that he will woo them back. Continue to love the wayward child lavishly and to pray continually, trusting God to complete the work he began in your children when you started them off "on the way they should go."

Lord, I'm grateful you love my loved ones far more than I do and that you are pursuing them, amen.

People look at the outward appearance, but the Lord looks at the heart.
1 SAMUEL 16:7

"The LORD does not look at the things people look at. People look at the outward appearance, but the LORD looks at the heart."

1 SAMUEL 16:7

Samuel was on a mission from God: he was to go to the family of Jesse and anoint the son whom the Lord instructed him to name as king over Israel.

So the prophet Samuel looked over the sons of Jesse, and God selected . . . none of them. Only when the prophet asked Jesse if he had any other sons did Samuel learn that David, the youngest, was out in the fields tending sheep. At Samuel's instruction, Jesse summoned David, and when David came in, God let Samuel know that he would be Israel's next king.

What message does God have for us in this story? One takeaway is this: we live in a world hyper-obsessed with appearance. Only certain people have "the look," and only they "win" at life. On the outside they may indeed look like they have everything, but God looks at the heart and measures character.

Lord, please help me keep my heart pure and wholly devoted to you, amen.

*I know that the LORD secures justice for the
poor and upholds the cause of the needy.*

PSALM 140:12

The psalmist says, "I know." He had experienced God's justice. He had observed
the way God stands up for those who could
not defend themselves. The psalmist knew
that God sides with the oppressed.

Yet we may struggle in the world today to
see the Lord as the Advocate of the downtrodden. It's hard to see the hand of God at
work in so much suffering. But we cannot see
as he does. In the chaos, we cannot see the
stories he's bringing to God-glorifying closure.

The truth is, God is at work behind the
scenes, and he will inevitably right the wrongs
and bring ultimate justice to the world.

Even so, as we wait and as suffering continues, we must pray for our world, asking God
for his just and perfect will to happen on earth
as it is accomplished in heaven.

*Lord, please work on behalf of the poor and
the broken. Help me to see them, too, so that
you can use me in your efforts. I want to
be part of your work in their lives, amen.*

*As iron sharpens iron, so one
person sharpens another.*

PROVERBS 27:17

We Christ followers need each other—
that's the heartbeat of today's verse.
We cannot grow spiritually in isolation. Hiding
out in a mountain cabin will never help us
become the people God wants us to be. He
designed us to be in relationship—with him
and with others. One of the good things that
happens in such a community of believers is
sharpening each other.

When you want to sharpen a knife, you
need another piece of metal called a sharpening stone. You can't use wood or glass to
sharpen a knife. It needs a similar form to
make it sharp, and that is true for us. We need
each other to smooth our rough edges (which
we may be blind to) and sharpen our effec-
tiveness for when we serve in God's kingdom.

Yes, metal on metal can mean sparks fly.
And that's okay. Consider it progress!

*Lord, please put people in my life who will keep
me sharp and make me sharper—and use me
to sharpen them, all for your glory, amen.*

*"Do not judge, and you will not be judged.
Do not condemn, and you will not be
condemned. Forgive, and you will be forgiven."*

LUKE 6:37

Here, Jesus issued three commands: "Don't judge. Don't condemn. Do forgive." And the result of your obedience? You won't be judged. You won't be condemned. You will be forgiven.

First, Jesus called us to not criticize, look for others' sins, or put ourselves in the place of God and pronounce someone guilty. The judgment of human souls is God's job and his alone. We are not to judge, but we are to humbly and wisely exercise discernment about the behavior of our brothers and sisters and then enact church discipline when necessary.

Similarly, we are not to condemn. We can come alongside a Christ follower whose behavior concerns us, but we cannot know that person's heart. Only God can, so only he is in a position to condemn.

We are, however, to forgive, to—like Jesus—extend grace, forgive those who hurt us, and glorify God as we do so. Jesus gave his life to secure our forgiveness so we should forgive others.

*Lord, help me to stop judging and condemning
others. Enable me to forgive, amen.*

*Jesus Christ is the same yesterday
and today and forever.*

HEBREWS 13:8

*O*ur lives are in constant flux. We live somewhere for a while, only to move to an unfamiliar place. Or our jobs shift. Or friends move away. Or our relationships change as we navigate a changing interpersonal landscape. Even our bodies change as we age. Nothing seems to stay the same.

Nothing except Jesus Christ. Today's Scripture proclaims his unchangeableness. He is consistently good, steady, strong, kind, and loving. His promises will never be revoked. The death he suffered on the cross has enabled you to know him intimately.

So when your life swirls into chaos, when circumstances change before your eyes, take courage in knowing your very patient Savior remains the same. He who flung the stars into existence will carry you when your life feels flung in a hundred different directions. In addition, he knows you. He knows what is best for your life. And he will be there for you and with you each step of the way.

*Lord, I so need to know your steadiness
today. I need you, my unchanging God,
when life spins out of control, amen.*

August

SPEAK, my lord, SINCE YOU HAVE GIVEN ME strength.

DANIEL 10:19

*"Do not be afraid, you who are
highly esteemed," he said. "Peace!
Be strong now; be strong."
When he spoke to me, I was strengthened and said,
"Speak, my lord, since you have given me strength."*

DANIEL 10:19

Maybe it's subtle to some, the difference between hearing and listening. Here's one way to make the distinction: hearing is what happens when sound waves hit an eardrum; listening is what happens when the heart and mind are involved.

And we can find it hard to listen when we are fearful, annoyed, worried, hungry, preoccupied, stressed out, or trying to make a decision. We can also find it hard to listen when we are exhausted, as Daniel was.

When a man dressed in linen appeared to Daniel in a vision, the words he spoke renewed Daniel's strength. And the God who sent that man to Daniel has given you and me words that can renew our strength. We find those words in Scripture.

Open your heart as you open its pages and find strength for today.

*Lord, thank you for your Word that renews our
strength and, with that, our ability to listen
to your instructions and encouragement.*

August 2

*The warden paid no attention to
anything under Joseph's care, because
the Lord was with Joseph and gave
him success in whatever he did.*

GENESIS 39:23

Joseph foreshadowed the One who was to come: Jesus Christ. Joseph was an archetype of a suffering servant. At the same time, Joseph was a living, breathing man who grieved and sweat and hurt and rejoiced. The hallmark of Joseph's life was the fact that God was with him.

Joseph was a man of integrity, but—according to God's plan—he found himself in all kinds of tough situations. Each time and in his own timing, God intervened for Joseph. God did prosper him—but he didn't protect or immediately deliver Joseph from various trials.

All these trials, though, were seasons of growth for Joseph. The bravado he had as a youth morphed into steady faithfulness to God and genuine humility.

Whatever hardships you encounter, may you—like Joseph—stay faithful to God and confident that he intends those hardships for ultimate good.

*Lord, in the midst of my trials today,
I choose to trust that you have
everything under control, amen.*

The good shepherd lays down his life for the sheep.

JOHN 10:11

"I am the good shepherd. The good shepherd lays down his life for the sheep."

JOHN 10:11

A bad shepherd lets his sheep to stray. He neglects the flock, allowing the sheep to graze in bad fields or experience life-threatening thirst. He beats the lambs to teach submission and obedience. He isn't alert to predators, allowing them to get too close to the sheep. Clearly, he doesn't care much about the welfare of his sheep.

But Jesus is the opposite, rightly calling himself the good Shepherd. When a sheep strays, he goes out looking for that wanderer, searching until he finds it and rejoicing when he does. He stays up during the watches of the night, listening for predators, watching the shadows for movement, protecting his flock from lions and bears. He leads the sheep to green pastures and, according to Psalm 23, to still waters where they can drink. Speaking quietly, he gently guides his flock that willingly follows. This good Shepherd finds joy in how well his sheep are doing.

You, dear one, are a lamb in the care of the good Shepherd.

Lord, I'm so grateful to be in your flock, to have you, the good Shepherd, taking care of me, amen.

*All of them were filled with the Holy
Spirit and began to speak in other
tongues as the Spirit enabled them.*

ACTS 2:4

All of them. Every single person waiting in the Upper Room was praying, singing, waiting, trusting—and all of them received the Spirit of God. The Spirit came with tongues as of fire and the sound of a violent wind, fell upon them, and enabled them to speak in other languages—and the words they spoke were in praise to God (v. 11).

What is your praise level today? Have you reached your saturation point? Of course not! None of us can reach a perfect or adequate amount of praise—and that's not to be a goal. But if praising God indicates the presence of the Spirit of God within a person, what evidence that God's Spirit is with you did you see in the past week? This past month? May God's Spirit with you fuel joy and prompt heartfelt praise!

Even if life is dark and hard, you can still choose right now to take your eyes off your circumstances, look to God, and to praise his goodness anyway.

*Lord, I want to choose to praise
you today, amen.*

The Son of MAN did not COME TO BE SERVED, BUT TO SERVE. Mark 10:45

"Even the Son of Man did not come to be served, but to serve, and to give his life as a ransom for many."

MARK 10:45

Jesus is the King and Creator of the universe. He fashioned everything you see—the cosmos, the solar system, our earth; mountains, deserts, oceans; and every single person who has walked this planet. He is worthy of our reverence and awe, our respect and devotion.

You would think that when he came to earth, he would have enjoyed the privileges of royalty. But Jesus took "the very nature of a servant" and "humbled himself by becoming obedient to death" (Philippians 2:7–8). He came to show how we all should live—as servants. Jesus served in many ways, healing the sick, freeing the demoniac, enabling the lame to walk and the blind to see, and raising the dead. Jesus taught the Pharisee, the Samaritan woman, and common Jewish fishermen. And in his ultimate act as a Servant, Jesus died on the cross, ransoming you from eternal death.

Live out your gratitude by serving as your Lord served.

Lord, give me your perspective on this world: show me whom you would have me serve in your name, amen.

When Daniel learned that the decree had been published, he went home to his upstairs room where the windows opened toward Jerusalem. Three times a day he got down on his knees and prayed, giving thanks to his God, just as he had done before.

DANIEL 6:10

Daniel was faithful to his God. He, for instance, worshipped God at different times throughout his day, and he didn't stop doing so when such prayer was outlawed.

Daniel is a great inspiration for all of us. Even though our lives are busy, we can choose to worship God several times a day just as Daniel did. We can read God's Word, pray as we go about our day, sing worship songs, serve others, or spend time alone listening for God's voice. Develop holy habits like these that will work for you and enable you to stay in touch with God.

Do this, and then when life hits hard, you'll already be in the habit of following, loving, and trusting God—just as Daniel was.

Lord, help me develop habits that keep me vitally connected to you throughout my day, amen.

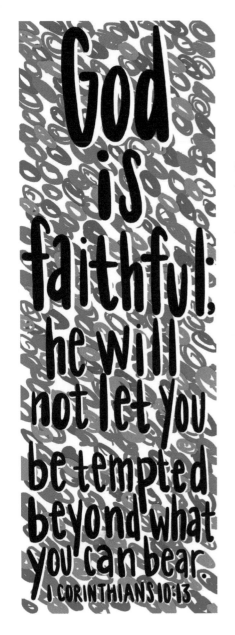

God is faithful;
he will not let you
be tempted
beyond what
you can bear.
1 CORINTHIANS 10:13

God is faithful; he will not let you be tempted beyond what you can bear. But when you are tempted, he will also provide a way out.

1 CORINTHIANS 10:13

The first three words of this verse set forth a truth we can build our lives on: God *is* faithful. The sun rises and sets. He keeps your heart beating. You have forgiveness through Jesus and a gospel purpose in life. God is utterly and always faithful.

And your faithful God will help you when you face temptations by providing a way of escape. God is never behind the temptations, but he always enables you to resist them or escape them.

We have to want to be helped in resisting those temptations, however. Look back on your life. When have you accessed the path of escape from temptation that God gave you? And when have you ignored it? How did you feel in the aftermath of each decision?

The Lord wants good things for you—freedom from shame, for example—and that's why he provides you with an escape from every temptation you find yourself facing.

Lord, when temptation comes my way,
please help me recognize the escape
you provide and use it, amen.

"I am the vine; you are the branches. If you remain in me and I in you, you will bear much fruit; apart from me you can do nothing."

JOHN 15:5

We human beings don't do well if we're not living with a sense of purpose. We want to make a difference—or, to use Jesus' words, we want to "bear much fruit." What Jesus taught here is that we can do nothing of eternal value without him. We will make no eternal impact if we are doing things in our own strength.

So Jesus' call to you today is to abide or remain in him. He explained with an example from nature: Jesus is the vine that provides the lifeblood to you, the branch attached to that vine. You must stay connected to him, or death and decay will come.

If you want to have a truly fruitful life, abide in Jesus: spend your time loving him, listening for his voice, adoring him in worship, and imploring him through prayer. When you do, your life will indeed bear much fruit.

Lord, I want to bear fruit for you, so please help me to abide in you today, amen.

We have only ONLY FIVE loaves of BREAD & TWO fish.

LUKE 9:13

We have only five loaves of bread and two fish.

LUKE 9:13

*L*ittle is much in the hands of Jesus.

The crowd of five thousand men—plus women and children—was hungry. The situation could have gotten volatile as the people grew hungrier and impatient, as tiredness led to crankiness. In the crowd was a young boy with his lunch, five little loaves of bread and two dried fish. But Jesus took that little and made it much. With those small amounts, he satisfied the hunger of a crowd of thousands after the boy willingly shared what he had, and the disciples acted on their initially meager faith.

Don't miss this encouraging truth! We can approach God with "But I have only _____" and hear him say, "That's okay. It is enough. Simply place in my hands what you have."

That's the key: surrender. Take the little you have and give it as an offering to Jesus. He can multiply your small amount and do something miraculous and satisfying. Take the small faith you have, place it in Jesus' hands, and watch him do something big.

Lord, I praise you that little is much in your hands, amen.

August 10

*Each of you should use whatever gift you
have received to serve others, as faithful
stewards of God's grace in its various forms.*

1 PETER 4:10

God gives every believer a unique gift or combination of gifts, not so any of us can brag, but so we can serve others. So rather than fretting about whether your gifts are as amazing as another person's or even at all noteworthy, spend your time thinking about how you can use those gifts to serve God by serving people.

If God has gifted you to teach, what opportunities has he opened up for you to serve others through your teaching? If God has given you administrative skills, what ministry would benefit from your help? If God has equipped you to believe him for great things, at what nonprofit can you serve as a volunteer?

God's design is truly beautiful! He made you unique, one-of-a-kind. And he gifted you with specific skills, abilities, talents, and passions that you can use to be a blessing to this world in his name.

*Lord, help me identify my gifts and then show
me where I can be of greatest service! Amen.*

Do NOT BE AFRAID. I AM the FIRST & THE LAST.

Revelation 1:17

"Do not be afraid. I am the First and the Last. I am the Living One; I was dead, and now look, I am alive for ever and ever!"

REVELATION 1:17–18

Jesus did exactly what he said he would do: he died for our sins, rose from death to life, and thereby obliterated the barrier of sin and the specter of death. That's the kind of Savior we can rely on. We can trust a Person who has conquered death.

And this trustworthy God is also at the beginning and the end of the story you're living on this earth. He formed you, fashioning your personality, physical traits, and heart. He was there when you took your first breath of air. In fact, he who conquered death will hold your heart and your hands now, when you face death in the future, and every moment in between.

The same power that raised Jesus from the dead—the power of the Holy Spirit—is alive in you today. In light of the Spirit's life within you, dare to trust Almighty God with every single circumstance in your life today.

Jesus, I choose to trust you, the reliable, powerful, victorious resurrected One, amen.

*If we confess our sins, he is faithful and
just and will forgive us our sins and
purify us from all unrighteousness.*

1 JOHN 1:9

What a marvelous promise! When we confess, God forgives and cleanses!

The context of this promise is John's statement that "God is light" (v. 5). We can enter that light—we can enjoy fellowship with our holy God—only if we have been cleansed of our sin. And we can be cleansed of our sin only if we confess it to God.

What can also help forgiveness be more real is to confess your sins to a fellow Christian whom you trust. Bringing that darkness into the light is what God instructs for your good—and then to receive a hug from the friend who still loves you after the confession is to taste God's unconditional love.

So—as John instructed—confess your sin. When you do, you begin to be free of it. The enemy's constantly nagging voice will be silenced, and God will continue his work to heal and restore.

*Lord, please show me the sin I need to
confess—and, when I need to, a safe
person to confess my sin to, amen.*

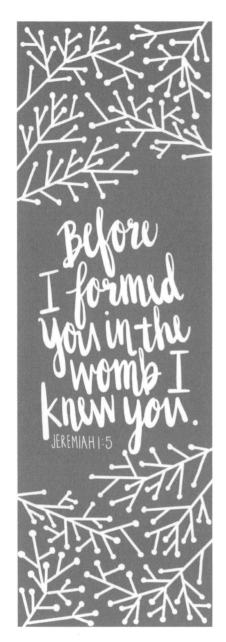

Before I formed you in the womb I knew you.

JEREMIAH 1:5

"Before I formed you in the womb I knew you, before you were born I set you apart."

JEREMIAH 1:5

*D*id you know that Jeremiah is some-times called "the weeping prophet"? He said things to the nation of Israel on God's behalf, things that made them angry. As a result, Jeremiah experienced heartache and isolation. He endured much pain at the hands of his own people, and he could have easily doubted God's goodness because of it.

But maybe when his ministry got rough, Jeremiah thought back to these words God spoke when he called the prophet into service. First, God had known Jeremiah even before he formed the prophet in his mother's womb. Second, God told Jeremiah that he had been set apart for a Jeremiah-shaped mission.

It's the same for you. God knew you before you were formed in the womb, and he has a very special you-shaped mission for you to fulfill. Send your roots deep into those truths today.

Lord, thank you for making me and for choosing me to do the me-shaped work you have designed for me to do, amen.

God is not a God of disorder but of peace.

1 CORINTHIANS 14:33

The early church was in its formative stages, and often instruction was in order. Such was the case when Paul wrote to the Corinthian believers. When they met together to worship, Paul told them, they must share "a hymn, or a word of instruction, a revelation, a tongue or an interpretation" (v. 26) in an orderly and peaceful manner that would effectively build up the church as well as reflect the order and peace of God. A time of worship was not to be chaotic, for such disarray would not accurately represent God or help people worship well.

Consider the value of order and peace during worship. Basically, we need worship to be about God, not about us. An orderly worship enables that to happen: we can focus on God so that he can change our hearts. We want to be different people after encountering God in worship, corporate or private, but always orderly.

Lord, thank you for the reminder that worship is to be all about you. Help that also to be true of my private worship times, amen.

"No weapon forged against you will prevail."

ISAIAH 54:17

*I*t is all too easy to live in fear, fretting about what will happen next in the world and our nation as well as in our communities, families, and personal life of family, ministry, and work. We may also worry about what the enemy of our souls is up to. Will Satan attack our family? Will he cause us to stumble and fall into sin? Will we see a child turn from the Lord?

The enemy of our souls may attempt to harm us, but today's promise from the book of Isaiah reminds us that nothing he does will prevail. His attacks may sideline us for a bit, break our hearts, and bewilder us. But Satan's work will not prosper.

If you're unsure, think for a minute about the God who protects you. He knows how to best shield you and defend you from the arrows of the evil one. He is smarter and stronger than Satan. Your good and powerful God will lead you through your current trial, no matter how difficult it is.

Lord, thank you that you won't allow Satan's attacks to prevail in my life, amen.

*May these words of my mouth and this
meditation of my heart be pleasing in your sight.*

PSALM 19:14

We should write down—better yet, we should memorize—the psalmist's words here. Why? Because it's so hard to keep our words and thoughts pure, isn't it? As we pray this verse with the psalmist, we remind ourselves just how much we need God to please him with our words and our thoughts.

Today, as you go about your day, ask God to help you choose words wisely and speak them kindly. Seek to build up someone who's frustrated. Instead of retaliating when someone bothers you, choose to bless that person. Instead of gossiping, find positive things to say about people.

As you pray about your words, also ask God to purify your heart and to make your motives right and God-honoring rather than springing from selfish ambition or a need to be noticed. Ask God to show you where he would have you serve others—and then do so for the sake of his fame, not yours.

*Lord, I do pray my words please you,
and I ask you to make my heart as well
as my words right today, amen.*

THE SPIRIT HIMSELF TESTIFIES WITH OUR SPIRIT THAT WE ARE GOD'S CHILDREN.

ROMANS 8:16

The Spirit himself testifies with our spirit that we are God's children.

ROMANS 8:16

*Y*ou are God's sweet child. Think about that. Maybe your folks are alive, or maybe they have passed. Maybe you grew up in a home where a parent neglected or harmed you. But having named Jesus your Savior and Lord, you will never be parentless. Your heavenly Father calls you and welcomes you into his family.

Everything a good parent does, God the Father does. He watches your progress. He sings songs of joy over you. He disciplines you so your soul will prosper and you'll become mature and wise. He protects and provides for you. He blesses you with good relationships. He sets you on your own two feet after rescuing you from sin and healing you.

Oh, child of God, how loved you are! Whatever you do today, whatever you think, however far away you run, this bedrock truth remains: you are loved by your Father. Settle yourself into his wide embrace today. Rest there. Be loved, beloved.

Lord, thank you for being my heavenly Father and perfect parent. Thank you for loving me my whole life through, amen.

If you fail to do this, you will be sinning against the LORD; and you may be sure that your sin will find you out.

NUMBERS 32:23

These are the words of Moses to the tribes of Reuben and Gad. Moses had just charged them with fighting for the promised land with the rest of Israel. Then came today's verse, which serves as a warning for all of us centuries later: God sees. This truth can be an amazing comfort when we're walking through a trial, but it can also be rather frightening because God sees us when we are sinning as well.

We cannot pull the wool over God's eyes. God knows that we can't keep our sins hidden forever and that our sins will destroy us.

The truth of today's verse, however, is also good news if you long for justice. You can be reassured that God sees all the evil in the world. Nothing escapes his notice, and he will eventually bring every guilty person to justice. God will see that all wrongs are punished and all acts of kindness are rewarded.

Lord, I praise you that your justice will prevail. Help me to live justly, not in sin, amen.

If someone dies, will they live again?

JOB 14:14

In the Old Testament, this was a legitimate question. When Jesus walked the earth, he ushered in the age of resurrection when he raised several people from the dead, including his good friend Lazarus.

And then Jesus himself was resurrected. The good news for you today is that because of Jesus' death on the cross and subsequent resurrection, you have hope that death is not the end.

What an amazing hope! And it's especially amazing for people like Job who desperately needed hope. The resurrection plays no favorites: eternal life with Christ after we die physically is possible because of the sacrifice of Jesus, and all are welcome to receive this gift.

Spend some time making a list of people you know who need to hear this beautiful invitation to life with Jesus. Pray for them. Then ask God to give you the opportunity as well as the courage to share this good news.

Lord, show me whom to talk with about the resurrection—and then give me, I pray, not only the opportunity but also bold and effective words, amen.

*Then will the eyes of the blind be opened
and the ears of the deaf unstopped.*

ISAIAH 35:5

*I*n these words about what would happen when the Messiah came, the prophet Isaiah gave faithful Jews a hint of what was to come.

Enter Jesus. Soon after performing his first miracle of turning water into wine at the wedding in Cana, Jesus began to fulfill this part of Isaiah's prophecy: he healed people who were born blind, he opened the ears of the deaf, he opened the mouths of the mute, and he raised people from the dead.

All these miracles were intended to be signs proving he was the long-awaited Messiah spoken about by the Old Testament prophets. As John the apostle noted in his gospel, though, "Jesus did many other things as well," but the world would not have enough room for all the books it would take to record all Jesus did (see John 21:25).

Today, Jesus continues to act on behalf of his followers. His complete power and perfect love mean you can live with hope and peace.

*Lord, thank you for doing miracles to show us
your divine power and life-changing love, amen.*

The LORD rewards everyone for their righteousness and faithfulness.

1 SAMUEL 26:23

This world doesn't always appreciate righteousness and faithfulness. Instead, it often rewards conniving, trickery, lies, and deceit, honoring those who take shortcuts.

The world's systems are transitory; its rewards, fleeting. Yes, people may get ahead in the short term: those who cheat and steal can seem to get away with it. White-collar criminals embezzle, predators abuse, and politicians give favors. But these people will not know God's rewards in heaven. He sees all, and they will be held accountable when they meet him.

In light of the world's upside-down values and cheap rewards, choose to live for an audience of One: choose to live in a way that honors and pleases Jesus Christ. Live with integrity, speak only truth, serve with humility, put other people's needs ahead of yours, share generously what God has blessed you with, talk to people about the Lord, and love others with God's love. Living rightly is indeed its own reward, but God also blesses his faithful ones with eternal rewards.

Lord, enable me to live a life of service characterized by humility, integrity, and love as a way of honoring you and loving you, amen.

This is how we know what love is: Jesus Christ laid down his life for us. And we ought to lay down our lives for our brothers and sisters.

1 JOHN 3:16

Jesus made the ultimate sacrifice when he laid down his life for us. Here's another picture of an ultimate sacrifice. You are blind and deaf, standing on a train track and completely unaware of the train roaring toward you. A bystander sees you there, oblivious to the danger, and runs toward you to push you out of harm's way, which she successfully does . . . only to lose her own life.

That's what Jesus has done for you. Pushing you out of harm's way, he took the full impact of the train on your behalf. What did John tell us to do in response? He encouraged us to love in the same sacrificial manner.

In short, when you inconvenience yourself for the sake of another, you act in a small way just like Jesus did.

Lord, open my eyes to the needs around me today. Make me willing to die to myself to help meet those needs, amen.

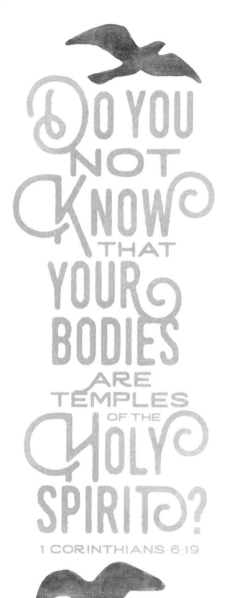

Do You Not Know That Your Bodies Are Temples Of The Holy Spirit?

1 CORINTHIANS 6:19

Do you not know that your bodies are
temples of the Holy Spirit, who is in you,
whom you have received from God?

1 CORINTHIANS 6:19

In the Old Testament, God dwelled among the Israelites in a cloud, fire, a tabernacle, and then the temple's Holy of Holies. God's people could point to the presence of God with them, but they could not enter the Holy of Holies without risking their lives.

When Jesus died, however, the veil that surrounded the Holy of Holies was torn in two, from top to bottom. What a picture of what Jesus did! God ripped the curtain from heaven downward, declaring that the way into his presence was now open.

And now—as the apostle Paul taught—our very bodies house God's glory. You have the very presence of God—the Holy Spirit—housed within you. What an amazing privilege and blessing!

If you feel far from God today, stop a moment and simply consider this profound truth. You are the house of God. The Holy Spirit abides inside you. And he always will.

Lord, I'm amazed that you live within me.
Help me realize how awesome that is, amen.

August 24

You make known to me the path of life; you will fill me with joy in your presence, with eternal pleasures at your right hand.

PSALM 16:11

What rich encouragement the psalmist's words offer us, especially those of us who are struggling.

First, the psalmist states that God will make known the path of life—the path of purpose and hope, forgiveness and redemption, new beginnings and eternal significance. God loves to help you revise the story of your life; he takes your brokenness, repairs your soul, and sets your feet on a straight path, on his path for your good and his glory.

God will also give you joy in his presence. Simply sit quietly and listen for his voice. Invite him to make his presence with you known. Joy will come in those quiet moments of reflection, especially as you begin to thank God for all the things he has done for you.

Finally, the pleasures God blesses you with are eternal. They are not trivial or temporary. And that is yet another reason you can sing for joy today.

Lord, I want to follow your path and know joy in your presence today and always, amen.

Then Abram gave him a tenth of everything.

GENESIS 14:20

*A*s this verse illustrates, Abram had a clear understanding of stewardship. He knew that God owned absolutely everything. In response to that, he made a commitment to give back to the Lord 10 percent of everything he had.

Why did Abram do this? Did God need his wealth? No. God owns everything and is master of all, of mountains, oceans, stars, and the universe. Abram gave this 10 percent to show his allegiance to God and to demonstrate his trust that, by God's grace, his house would not run out of food.

When we give as Abram gave, we loosen money's hold on our lives. We show that we trust more in God than our money. After all, like Abram, we have been given much by God so that we can become a blessing to many. And when we hold our possessions loosely, we'll give with greater joy, and we'll deepen our trust in the God who provides it all.

*Lord, I want to give joyfully. I acknowledge
that you own it all anyway. I trust you
to use my gifts for your glory and to
continue to provide for me, amen.*

August 26

"The Sovereign LORD says: I myself will search for my sheep and look after them."

EZEKIEL 34:11

This word from Ezekiel foreshadows Jesus' statement that he is the good Shepherd who lays down his life for the sheep, the one who leaves the ninety-nine to find the lost one (see John 10:11 and Luke 15:4). And we are indeed God's sheep—and that is not a compliment. Like bumbling sheep, we are hopelessly lost at times, we tend to wander the wilderness, and we aren't known for our courage and wisdom. Yet there is hope.

Our hope lies in our sovereign God, who is at the same time our shepherd. *Sovereign* means that God rules over the universe, the stars, the moon, and you and me. And as our Shepherd, he watches over all of us with care and compassion.

So whatever you're facing today, remember the power and the kindness of God, your sovereign Shepherd. Sometimes you need power, and other times, kindness. At times you'll need both in good measure. And he will always give you what you, his sheep, need.

Lord, please provide me with your power and the ability to share your compassion today, my sovereign Shepherd, amen.

*The LORD is close to the brokenhearted and
saves those who are crushed in spirit.*

PSALM 34:18

What an amazing promise! God comes near not to people who have it all together, not to those who always succeed, not to those whose hearts have never been broken. No, God comes close to those whose hearts are broken and whose spirits have been crushed by the weight of the world, the unfairness of life, or the very people they trusted.

God doesn't leave us alone in our loneliness. He isn't afraid of our pain. He doesn't try to say words to make it right, and he can handle our being angry at him. God draws near to us when we are hurting.

And in this fallen world populated by sinners, we can't avoid getting hurt. But God draws near to the brokenhearted. He will hold your hand while you're walking through the fire. He will be with you as you face relational heartache, physical pain, or worry about the future. He will come near. All you need to do is call upon him.

*Lord, I'm so very grateful that you
come near, that you don't leave me
alone when I need you, amen.*

*"He himself bore our sins" in his body
on the cross, so that we might die to
sins and live for righteousness; "by his
wounds you have been healed."*

1 PETER 2:24

We often read about Jesus dying on the cross, yet the impact of that act can be lost on us. What does it mean that Jesus bore our sins "in his body"? Consider this: Think of all the sins you have forgiven and know you need to forgive. Then see those sins tattooed across Jesus' shoulders: slander, malice, hatred, and harsh words.

Now consider your sins. Tattoo those on Jesus' shoulders too. Remember: Jesus didn't just bear those words; he took on the responsibility for the actual acts. He experienced abandonment. He heard words of betrayal.

All this Jesus did for you. His wounds—caused by the sins of everyone—are the means of your healed relationship with God, with your holy heavenly Father. It's an astounding thought. And it's the kind of truth that will set you free. Why? Because you are that loved.

*Lord, thank you for bearing my sins on the cross
so I can be in a relationship with you, amen.*

Submit yourselves, then, to God. Resist the devil, and he will flee from you. Come near to God and he will come near to you.

JAMES 4:7-8

*J*ames listed three actions in these highly packed verses: submit, resist, and come near.

To submit to God means to recognize that you are not in control of this world or even of your own world. But God is: your all-wise, all-loving God is in perfect control. And he knows what is best, so you can choose to give the reins of your life over to him.

To resist the devil is to remind yourself of God's Word, like Jesus did in the wilderness when he was tempted (see Matthew 4). When the devil throws lies your way, respond with the truth of Scripture and choose to live according to that truth.

To come near to God means that you make time to connect with him, asking for his help, insight, and strength. When you do that, he will bless you with his presence.

Lord, I choose today to submit to you, resist sin, and come near to you. I'm grateful for your presence in my life, amen.

Peter began to speak: "I now realize how true
it is that God does not show favoritism."

ACTS 10:34

Right before Peter said these words, he had seen a vision of unclean foods displayed before him on a sheet. All his life he had lived with dietary laws (don't eat this; do eat that) and racial prejudice (Gentiles are bad; don't associate with them).

But in a single encounter with the Lord in a vision, Peter learned that God was making a change. The once bad food was now considered clean, and—more importantly—Gentiles were being welcomed as God's people.

And this had been God's plan all along. His hope was that the nation of Israel would act like a city on a hill, drawing all nations to him. Unfortunately, this seldom happened. Even the disciples asked Jesus if he was going to finally restore the kingdom to Israel. Jesus' closest followers didn't realize that he had opened up the kingdom to the whole wide world, to the Gentiles. We who are not of Jewish blood are no longer unclean. Instead, we are welcomed into God's eternal kingdom.

Jesus, thank you for inviting me into your
kingdom. I am grateful to be included, amen.

*Whatever you do, work at it with all your heart,
as working for the Lord, not for human masters.*

COLOSSIANS 3:23

What were some of the first jobs you held? No matter what kind of work we do—paid or volunteer, a special project or an everyday chore, full-time or part-time—and whether we're passionate about it or not, we are always to work as if God were our boss.

That means as God's representatives, we do our work with excellence to bring him glory. We are to be wise stewards of this job God has provided. We can work with diligence and creativity, reflecting how God made us in his image. We can pour out our lives for the people we're working with, loving them with Jesus' love and doing our job with a servant's heart. We can view the profession as place to serve God and further his kingdom.

Wherever you work, know that God has placed you there strategically. Shine for him and serve him there. Remember that you are working for him.

*Lord, I want to work heartily for you,
whatever I'm doing, at home or in an office.
And may my work give you glory, amen.*

September

*Shortly before dawn Jesus went out
to them, walking on the lake.*

MATTHEW 14:25

No one else in the history of the world has ever walked on water in his own power because it's totally impossible. The heaviness of the human body cannot stay on the surface of the water.

Yet the God we serve is not stopped or even slowed down by the seeming impossible. The infinite God of the Bible stooped, came in human flesh to this earth, to show us how to live and love, and—as the supreme act of love—died on the cross for our sins. While he was here, this God-man often overrode natural law by healing the lame and the blind, feeding big crowds with small snacks, and, yes, walking on water.

The only One who could override the laws of nature would be the One who established those laws in the first place. So, acting on his great love for us, Jesus the Son of God took on human flesh. His death showed us his humanity, and—like his walking on water—his resurrection showed us his divinity.

*Lord, thank you who are the God-man for
dying and for rising from death, amen.*

*[God] has given us his very great and
precious promises, so that through
them you may participate in the divine
nature, having escaped the corruption
in the world caused by evil desires.*

2 PETER 1:4

When God promises something, he will always come through. You can trust what he says, and you can rely on his being faithful to his promises.

God, for instance, promised to bless the nation of Israel—which he ultimately did when he sent Jesus Christ as an unexpected kind of King. God also promised to remove our heart of stone and give us a heart of flesh, a new heart that longs to do what he wants us to do. God promised to save us from our sin, give us the Holy Spirit, and enable us to live godly lives.

You can absolutely rely on God's promises. After all, many of them have already been fulfilled in Jesus Christ. And know that the promised Holy Spirit is within you. He will enable you to withstand trials and temptations as you wait for the fulfillment of other promises God has made.

*Lord, thank you that you are a Promise
Maker and a Promise Keeper! Amen.*

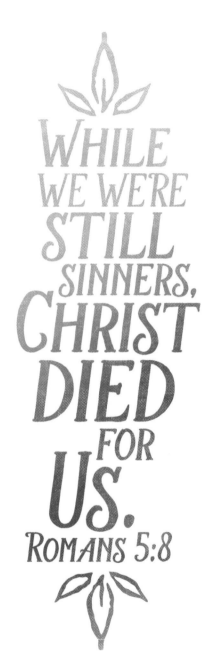

God demonstrates his own love for us in this:
While we were still sinners, Christ died for us.

ROMANS 5:8

What indescribable love God has for us! God showed—with the gift of his Son's very life—his affection and compassion for a group of folks who wanted nothing to do with him, who actively found ways to rebel against him. As King of the universe, he could have let us go our own way or destroyed us, but instead he chose to love us. And he showed his love by sacrificing his Son on our behalf.

And all history is marked by this remarkable act of sacrifice. No matter what your emotions tell you about God, especially when life is disappointing, the indisputable fact of God's kindness was demonstrated when Jesus hung on the cross.

Jesus didn't die for those deserving or worthy of his love. Instead, totally undeserving of God's wrath, Jesus died for those who didn't even comprehend what his sacrifice was accomplishing.

You don't need to fret about your standing before him. Your place has been made secure by his outrageous love.

Lord, thank you for loving me before
I even knew I needed it, amen.

Now to him who is able to do immeasurably
more than all we ask or imagine, according
to his power that is at work within us, to
him be glory . . . for ever and ever! Amen.

EPHESIANS 3:20–21

God's ways can far exceed our wildest expectations. We easily forget this, though, and ask him for smaller, ordinary things. Yet God calls us to a great adventure!—God supplies greater answers to prayer than we ever expected.

How can this be? Paul explained that it's the power of God that works within us. His Holy Spirit lives and breathes and walks with us throughout our lives. He gives us his power so, in his strength, we can do great things.

Yes, life is hard. But even when we are in difficult places, let's remember to dream. Let's keep our vision for what God can do broad and far-reaching. The Gospels show us just how astounding God's work can be. Jesus raised people from the dead, enabled the blind to see, freed the lame to dance, and gave dignity to the poor. Our prayers can unleash the limitless power of God!

Lord, enlarge my dreams for your
kingdom. I know you will answer in
powerful and amazing ways, amen.

*Cast all your anxiety on him
because he cares for you.*

1 PETER 5:7

Has anxiety bothered you this week? Have deadlines and to-do lists increased stress like bunnies multiplying in springtime? Have you noticed that the older you get, the more anxious you become? If you answered yes to any of those questions, look again at Peter's reminder of a very simple (but hard to do) solution: casting.

To cast is to throw something with such strength that you don't expect to have that object returned. Casting your anxiety, then, is an act of surrender. You can safely cast your cares on Jesus because he loves you. He is not sitting in heaven tsk-tsking you for being needy.

No, Jesus willingly bears your burdens. Compelled by his great love for you, he wants to take those worries and concerns from you. So your job is to let him do his job. Pray. Tell him about every single source of stress in your life. It's time to let your fear go into his the capable hands of your Friend.

*Jesus, please help me surrender my anxieties
to you. I am so grateful that you love me
and will take them from me, amen.*

*The fruit of the Spirit is love, joy, peace,
forbearance, kindness, goodness,
faithfulness, gentleness and self-control.*

GALATIANS 5:22–23

Read over this list of the fruit of the Spirit again, this time considering the impact each one could have on our relationships. After all, these gifts aren't best experienced in isolation. In fact, some are experienced only in community.

It's also important to notice that these Christlike qualities are ours for the asking. Since we who follow Jesus have the Holy Spirit within us, then these qualities are ours through him—and they are ours to live out in our relationships with others.

Take a minute to look back over your life. Are you more patient with people than you were five years ago? Are you kinder to family members who bother you? Do you keep your word and faithfully carry out your promises? If so, then you are growing in Christlikeness. If, however, you realize you're not seeing growth, ask God for a reset. Press into him, asking him to transform your character and make you more like Jesus.

*Lord, I'm grateful for these gifts. Continue to
grow them in me so that you may be reflected
in my interactions with others, amen.*

A gentle answer turns away wrath,
but a harsh word stirs up anger.

PROVERBS 15:1

The book of Proverbs offers us much practical information for life, especially for navigating relationships. Consider the importance of our reactions in a conversation. Our reactions matter because they often prompt what happens next—either the de-escalation of emotion or the fueling of tempers. First, an example of de-escalation.

A grade-school child hollers at you, and you choose to *not* respond in kind. You lower your voice, get down on his level, and speak gently. Your approach soothes the angry child. Typically, in that situation, the child responds to your quiet gentleness by calming down.

Second, you are arguing with a relative who said something that infuriated you. You react— you retaliate—with unkind words and a raised voice. More often than not, your reaction causes greater anger, and the chain reaction of a nuclear meltdown is under way.

So you have the choice today and every day: respond with quiet grace or react with provocative anger. Which will you choose?

Lord, give me your strength to respond to
people with kindness and grace instead of
anger that wants to retaliate, amen.

Let us consider how we may spur one
another on toward love and good deeds.

HEBREWS 10:24

*I*n this passage, the author of Hebrews
reminded us how important it is for us
to spend time with like-minded believers. We
must choose to make an effort and spend
time with people who sharpen us and encourage us in our walk with Christ.

But the sharpening and encouragement
need to go both ways. As we hang out with
awesome people, we're to be part of their
life change as well. We are to encourage the
people in our lives to love others and to do
good to them.

One way we encourage people is to
let them know when they're doing well.
Sometimes, though, we go first and, by our
example, encourage others to live well and
love well. As all of us strive to live like Jesus,
we are encouraging one another to keep at it.

So consider today how you might encourage someone toward good deeds—possibly
by doing some yourself.

Lord, thank you for my friends. Use any
good deeds I do today to encourage them
"toward love and good deeds," amen.

Jesus looked at [his disciples] and said, "With man this is impossible, but with God all things are possible."

MATTHEW 19:26

We do not control the cloud cover, and few of us understand the complex structure of the human heart. We don't have supernatural strength or knowledge or wisdom. But God possesses all these qualities and more. No wonder things that aren't possible for us are possible with God.

What situation or relationship that you are struggling with today seems impossible to resolve? What weight is proving too heavy for you to carry alone? Is someone you love needing to be delivered from an addiction? Does your paycheck fail to stretch far enough to cover your bills? These matters may seem huge, even impossible, but they are small to our big, our all-powerful God.

Spend some time today telling him about your cares, frustrations, worries, and burdens. Ask him to please intervene in miraculous ways. Do this with all the faith you can muster. Jesus honors our faith in him even when it is as small as a mustard seed.

Lord, I trust you to do the impossible today, amen.

*Let perseverance finish its work so that
you may be mature and complete.*

JAMES 1:4

What comes to mind when you hear the word *perseverance?* Maybe you think about hanging in when marriage is tough, the job is hardly satisfying, or the financial pressure isn't easing up. These are some of the trials we can encounter in a fallen world, and James was talking about such trials when he offered this encouragement.

To better understand the point James was making, read the context of today's verse: "Consider it pure joy, my brothers and sisters, whenever you face trials of many kinds, because you know that the testing of your faith produces perseverance" (vv. 2–3). Life's trials are both the training ground and the testing ground for our faith.

So, amid trials, may we choose the perspective of faith and remind ourselves that our God is sovereign and wise. As gym members say, "No pain, no gain." The pain of life's trials can yield the gain of spiritual maturity and strength.

*Lord, it's hard to endure these trials. I trust
you to give me strength and help me persevere
as—however counterintuitive it seems—you
use these days to grow my faith in you, amen.*

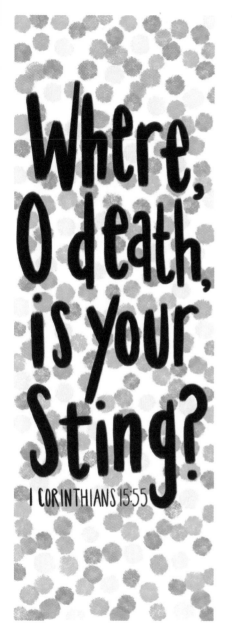

Where, O death, is your victory?
Where, O death, is your sting?

1 CORINTHIANS 15:55

September 11

In talking about the resurrection and Jesus' power over death, Paul shared these two rhetorical questions originally asked in the Old Testament. These questions had remained relevant, and now—after the death and resurrection of Jesus—everyone could know the definitive answers:

Where is death's victory? It is gone.

Where is death's sting? It no longer exists.

Why doesn't death have power over us? Because Jesus vanquished death, conquering it through his resurrection. Forgiven and cleansed of our sins, we now have access to God, to his presence and his power, and to eternal life with him in heaven.

So, when you walk through the valley of the shadow of death with a loved one, keep these truths in mind. Death will be sad, but its sting has been removed. Death may seem like the victor, but only for a moment.

*Lord, thank you for conquering death
so I no longer have to be afraid of
it or of what follows it, amen.*

*"The thief comes only to steal and kill
and destroy; I have come that they may
have life, and have it to the full."*

JOHN 10:10

When Jesus talked about the thief, he used vivid images to describe the work of Satan. After all, Satan's main goal on earth is to trip up believers. He wants to steal our hope, murder our spirits, and destroy our testimonies.

We should not underestimate the strength or the variety of our enemy's ways.

At the same time, we should not overestimate them either.

Today's verse, uttered by Jesus, reminds us that he is far more powerful than the devil: Satan's attempts to "steal and kill and destroy" will be overpowered by Jesus' ability to give life.

Yes, it's true that you have a very real enemy—but it's also wonderfully true that you have a God who is bigger and stronger than that enemy, a God who is capable of giving you a life overflowing with his joy, peace, and love.

*Lord, thank you that you are more powerful
than my enemy. And I thank you even more
that you give me life that is abundant in
your joy and peace, and love, amen.*

"Greater love has no one than this: to lay down one's life for one's friends."

JOHN 15:13

Jesus was nearing his appointment with death when he said these words to his disciples, and he made this statement for two reasons.

First, Jesus wanted to prepare these men for the challenge they would soon face: life without him. Jesus' crucifixion would not make sense because they expected him to defeat Rome and usher in a new but eternal kingdom. Certainly this King of an eternal kingdom would not die!

But this King did die.

Jesus also said these words of John 15:13 to remind his disciples about the why of the cross. Jesus died on the cross and rose from the dead, enabling forgiven human beings to be in relationship with holy God. And now God would become friends with mankind.

Jesus started this series of events, and he did so simply because he loved humanity. He laid down his life for us, whom he calls his friends.

Lord, your death on the cross was an amazing demonstration of your great love. I am so blessed to be loved by you, amen.

Take delight in the LORD, and he will
give you the desires of your heart.

PSALM 37:4

*D*elight and *desires.* Two great words, right? What does it mean to "take delight in the Lord"? According to the Merriam-Webster Dictionary, *delighting* means having "a strong feeling of happiness, great pleasure or satisfaction; something that makes you very happy." Your relationship with God should be a source of great happiness and pleasure. If that's not the case—if you feel distant from God or robotic in your relationship with him— perhaps it's time to take a little retreat and give yourself the opportunity to recapture the joy and excitement of your initial love for Jesus.

When we make God our supreme focus and learn the art of delighting in him, he has easy access to our hearts. As he works there to make us more like Jesus, he conforms the desires of our hearts to his desires for us. Then, when he gives you the desires of your heart, he is actually giving you what he desires for you.

Lord, I choose to delight in you today,
looking forward to your work in my heart
to make me more like Jesus, amen.

*"Come with me by yourselves to a
quiet place and get some rest."*

MARK 6:31

Jesus said these kind words to the disciples who must have been worn out from all their journeying. He invited them into a place of solitude and quiet after they all had been pressed into crowds, involved in countless conversations, and surrounded by loud voices. And Jesus wasn't asking them to do something that he hadn't already demonstrated. Many times the disciples had seen Jesus pull away to spend time alone with his Father.

This kind of quiet, rest, and prayer that Jesus modeled is essential for the Christ follower. Without it, we end up rushing and stressed out, of no use to anyone.

What prevents you from pulling away to be alone with God today? Is he calling you away to a quiet place because you need to be refreshed by rest? Instead of pushing against the invitation, accept it and welcome the respite. We finite human beings need the kindness and refreshment that our infinite God provides.

*Lord, I'm tired. So, so tired. Thank
you for inviting me to rest and
quietness in your presence, amen.*

"The kingdom of heaven is like treasure hidden in a field. When a man found it, he hid it again, and then in his joy went and sold all he had and bought that field."

MATTHEW 13:44

*I*n this verse, there's a three-letter word that's easy to miss. So focused on the treasure or the man's amazing sacrifice, we overlook *joy*. Let's consider its importance.

First, the kingdom of heaven truly is the greatest treasure imaginable. It is so valuable that we find sheer joy in giving up everything we have for its sake. In the same way, Jesus paid an immeasurably high price—like one that would be paid for a treasure—in order to usher us into his kingdom. Again, that kingdom is so valuable that we find great joy as we surrender everything to lay hold of it.

Such surrendering is not painful. In light of the kingdom treasures—of the eternal life, forgiveness of sin, and grace we receive—we can find it sheer joy to lay down our lives. And of course our greatest kingdom treasure is Jesus himself.

Lord, thank you that your kingdom brings joy, even in the sacrifices and surrender by which we obtain that treasure. Amen.

*We must go through many hardships
to enter the kingdom of God.*

ACTS 14:22

Sometimes we seem to think that God owes us an easy life. Or that being a Christian means we should escape hardship. Paul and Barnabas clarify the matter: It's not that Christians escape problems when they follow Christ. It's that Jesus is with us through those trials.

Suffering and persecution are normative for those who follow Jesus. Why? Because the enemy of our souls, Satan, immediately sees us as a target when we bend the knee and surrender our lives to God.

The good news is that our strong Jesus has already defeated Satan. Jesus conquered sin, death, and Satan when he rose from the dead. Our job on this earth, then, is to resist Satan, standing firm on the truth that the kingdom we serve is not of this world.

You may feel defeated right now. You may be facing hardship and pain. Persevere! Keep giving your worries and burdens over to God. And remember that Jesus is with you through the hardships and trials.

Lord, help me be aware of your presence with me when I face hardships and trials, amen.

September 18

*"I will establish the throne of
his kingdom forever."*

2 SAMUEL 7:13

*D*id you know that fifteen years passed between the prophet Samuel anointing David king of Israel and his finally sitting on the throne?

When the kingdom came to him, David didn't rule perfectly. In one gigantic lapse into sin, he committed both adultery and murder, and the aftermath of that sin marred the remaining years of David's kingship. In total, David reigned for forty years. Clearly—from a human perspective—his throne didn't last forever.

Yet in today's verse the Lord—speaking through the prophet Samuel—told of establishing a king who will reign forever. God was referring to Jesus' eventual and eternal throne. Jesus was born in the family line of David, and, like David, Jesus had to wait to be king. But unlike David, Jesus did not sin, and unlike David, Jesus will reign forever.

And, as a follower of Jesus, you are now part of his glorious and eternal kingdom.

*Lord, thank you for being the perfect King and
for welcoming me into your kingdom, amen.*

But Lot's wife LOOKED BACK, & she became a PILLAR of SALT.

GENESIS 19:26

*But Lot's wife looked back, and
she became a pillar of salt.*

GENESIS 19:26

Lot's wife was warned! The angel's instructions were clear: don't turn and look back at the destruction of Sodom and Gomorrah, at God's judgment of those corrupt cities. But something compelled her to turn. Was it hard to leave where she had been so comfortable? Was she worried about friends or loved ones? Did she need closure of some kind? Maybe she was just curious, but no one else looked back. Whatever her reasons were, this woman's choice to disobey had dire consequences. It cost her, her life.

In the New Testament, Jesus issued the same warning illustrated by Lot's wife: "No one who puts a hand to the plow and looks back is fit for service in the kingdom of God" (Luke 9:62). We can't look back and move forward at the same time. We will veer off the path Jesus has for us. We will plow a crooked row.

So look forward as you move ahead on the path your faithful God has called you to.

*Lord, I want to move forward, trusting
you for what's next, amen.*

The unfolding of your words gives light;
it gives understanding to the simple.

PSALM 119:130

Psalm 119—from verse 1 all the way to verse 176—is a tribute to God's Word. If you're ever doubting your faith or struggling with your beliefs, turn to this psalm. According to this snippet, God's Word illuminates. It sheds its light of truth and helps us see things clearly.

In a world of ever-increasing darkness and confusion, where right is wrong and wrong is right, God's Word can serve as a stabilizing force. It anchors us to what is true. It shines light on our circumstances, speaks to our hearts, helps us figure out our motives, and gives us direction for our lives.

Then, the second part of today's verse offers this great promise: if we lack wisdom, God's Word will give us profound understanding about how life works and how best to navigate it.

So if you find yourself confused or worried about the future, dig into God's Word. God loves to speak to you through its pages, providing you with understanding and kingdom truth.

Lord, I look forward to hearing from
you as I immerse myself in your
amazing Word today! Amen.

Abram fell facedown, and God said to him,
"As for me, this is my covenant with you:
You will be the father of many nations."

GENESIS 17:3–4

It's not often we see patriarchs lying prostrate before someone. But here we see Abram's awe of the God who called him. In God's presence, all Abram could do was prostrate himself as God spoke miraculous words over him. Not only would Abram have a child, but this child would one day be a nation that would give birth to many nations.

In light of such a forecast for his future, you might think Abram would be wrestling with pride. But instead of reveling in God's surprising words, Abram's response was to fall on his face and worship.

You may be facing what seems like an impossible situation. Take heart! Remember that you serve the God of the impossible. Whether or not he delivers you from your situation when and how you'd like him to, choose to worship him, preferring his presence with you over his presents to you.

Lord, may your goodness and your
good promises to me prompt me to
worship you as Abram did, amen.

September 22

*Who knows but that you have come to your
royal position for such a time as this?*

ESTHER 4:14

Queen Esther had a unique position in the Persian king's world: she found herself with the ability and opportunity to save her nation, the people of Israel. In today's Scripture, Mordecai reminded her of this truth. Though it must have been terrifying to intervene, Esther did—and her actions saved many from destruction.

What position are you in today? We forget that God has an amazing plan for our lives. We may wonder, *Why in the world am I here?* But the truth is, God is sovereign (he rules over everything), and his plan is perfect.

Right where you live, among the people you know, in your place of employment and ministry—this is where God has you . . . for such a time as this. Only you know these people. Only you have those unique connections. And you are integral to his plan. Like Esther, get involved in the story that God has written and watch him do amazing things.

*Lord, help me, like Esther, be open to what
you would have me do in my current
situation—and then enable me to act, amen.*

*But as for me and my household,
we will serve the Lord.*

JOSHUA 24:15

ear Joshua's bold pronouncement! A man of God, he knew whom he would serve! He also knew that many people in the nation of Israel were prone to turn away from God and that they needed to make a commitment to the one true God. He called them to throw away idols and turn away from pagan rituals. And in their presence, as their leader, he proclaimed his choice to follow the Lord.

We face that same choice in a world that is full of distractions. We can find ourselves serving money, leisure, fame, success, people, or our job—and neglecting to make our commitment to God our top priority. So you have a decision to make. Like Joshua, you can declare your choice to—in the power of the Holy Spirit—serve God with your whole heart. Will you?

Lord, I choose right now to serve you and you alone. Free me from the distractions and keep me focused on and devoted to you, amen.

"Peace I leave with you; my peace I give you. I do not give to you as the world gives. Do not let your hearts be troubled and do not be afraid."

JOHN 14:27

What beautiful words Jesus spoke over his disciples! He knew he would soon die on the cross, and he wanted the disciples to choose peace.

These words, while deeply encouraging, are something of a command. Jesus said he'll give us amazing peace. But in order to get the most out of that peace, let's follow Jesus' instructions here.

"Do not let your hearts be troubled." Life events can trouble us. When we notice the unsettledness, may we turn to Jesus, remember his sovereignty, and receive his peace.

"Do not be afraid." Fear grips many of us for numerous legitimate reasons. May we go to Jesus, let go of fear, and grab hold of all that Jesus has for us—especially his peace.

What a comfort to know Jesus cares enough for us to graciously, generously give us peace.

Lord, I don't want a troubled heart, and I choose not to give in to fear. May I instead receive your peace today, amen.

but they
could
not
stand
up
against
the
wisdom
the
Spirit
gave him
as he
spoke.
acts 6:10

[Jewish members of the synagogue]
could not stand up against the wisdom
the Spirit gave [Stephen] as he spoke.

ACTS 6:10

*D*id you know that the Greek word *mar-tys* means "witness"? When witnessing to God's truth and having faith in Jesus started costing people their lives, *martys* gave rise to our word *martyr*, a person who dies rather than denies his beliefs.

In Acts 6 we meet Stephen, a Greek-speaking Jew who spoke in the Greek-speaking synagogues of Jerusalem. He was also the first person martyred for his faith in Jesus. According to Acts 6:5, Stephen was "a man full of faith and of the Holy Spirit." Jewish leaders could not dispute his infuriating—yet Spirit-empowered, bold, articulate, scriptural, and wise—teachings.

The truths of Jesus Christ continue to infuriate today. The twenty-first-century world does not want to believe that there is only one way to God, but the Holy Spirit continues to empower twenty-first-century believers.

If you're skeptical, step out in faith and in obedience to the Spirit's guidance, and experience what Stephen did: the Spirit will provide wisdom and power.

Lord, may your Spirit enable me to speak clearly
and boldly the truth about Jesus, amen.

*He had no beauty or majesty to attract
us to him, nothing in his appearance
that we should desire him.*

ISAIAH 53:2

*K*ing Jesus, the long-awaited Messiah, was not what the nation of Israel expected.

In Jesus' day, the Jewish people were looking for a powerful king who would free them from Roman oppression. Focused on that, they had trouble making sense of Isaiah's words about the suffering servant.

When Jesus came on the scene, these words of Isaiah's prophecy proved true. An ordinary carpenter, growing up in the unremarkable town of Nazareth, Jesus didn't seek recognition from influential leaders who would back his cause. Instead, Jesus reached out to other ordinary people with words of truth, freedom, and love.

This is good news for you. Why? Because Jesus was ordinary, we can relate to him. Because he encountered in his earthly life all the things we face, he can be our trusted Friend. And know this truth: our ordinary Savior loves ordinary you extraordinarily.

*Lord, you may have looked ordinary to the
fishermen you hung around with, but you are
an extraordinary Savior! I love you, amen.*

Put on the full armor of God.

EPHESIANS 6:11

Put on the full armor of God, so that you can take your stand against the devil's schemes.

EPHESIANS 6:11

*A*nd what is the full armor of God? The belt of truth, the breastplate of righteousness, the gospel of peace, the shield of faith, the helmet of salvation, and the sword of the Spirit. We need all this armor to protect us from Satan, our wily enemy who schemes against us.

Satan longs for us to doubt God's goodness, so we shield ourselves from his lies and choose instead to live by faith in God's ability to take care of us. Satan's greatest defeat was the resurrection that ensured our salvation, and we revel in that beautiful and eternal deliverance. Last, we carry our offensive weapon, the Word of God—which is the very thing Jesus used to stand strong when the devil tempted him in the wilderness.

The battle is unseen but very real, as is our armor of God.

Lord, I thank you for providing the complete suit of armor and the only weapon I need to be protected from my enemy, amen.

*The LORD said, "I will cause all my goodness
to pass in front of you, and I will proclaim
my name, the LORD, in your presence."*

EXODUS 33:19

What must it have been like for Moses to have God's goodness pass in front of him? Was he terrified? Amazed? Silenced and in awe?

Not only did Moses see God in a way no one ever had, but earlier he had also heard God speak his own name.

What can you and I do to foster that kind of intimacy with God? Two words come to mind: *availability* and *submission*.

Moses spent time with God. As he led the nation of Israel through the wilderness, Moses knew he needed to rely on God for guidance, so Moses made himself available to his Lord. Then, after listening carefully to God's instructions, Moses submitted himself to the Lord: Moses chose to obey the Almighty.

Like Moses, you can experience greater intimacy with God when you make yourself available to him and then choose to submit to his guidance and will.

*Lord, I want to walk more closely to you.
Thank you for teaching me that availability
and submission are key, amen.*

small is the gate & narrow the road that leads to life.

MATTHEW 7:14

*"Small is the gate and narrow the road
that leads to life, and only a few find it."*

MATTHEW 7:14

We wish the road that leads to eternal life were easy, wide, and simple to navigate, but as Jesus taught, the way is narrow and few find it. Why is that? Isn't the gospel for anyone? Why don't more people find this narrow way?

The way is narrow because the toll to travel that road is humility. We have to recognize both our sinfulness and our utter inability to live a life of love and holiness. We can't rely on self-improvement programs or our own abilities to be right with God. We have to humble ourselves and admit we're lost without his forgiveness, his transforming work in our hearts, and his guidance and protection in our lives. And admitting these truths is not easy for us human beings who pride ourselves on our self-sufficiency.

The way is narrow, but humbly relinquishing control of our lives over to God means eternal life in the future and abundant life with him now.

*Lord, thank you for showing me
the narrow way and giving me the
humility to enter its gate, amen.*

*In him all things were created: things
in heaven and on earth, visible and
invisible, whether thrones or powers or
rulers or authorities; all things have been
created through him and for him.*

COLOSSIANS 1:16

Whenever you feel alone in the challenges, losses, and pain of life, remember this verse from Colossians. Consider that everything you see and touch and hear and smell was created by your amazing God. And your Creator God is keenly aware of all that happens in his world. That *all* includes you and your current situation.

Your heavenly Father knows why you are fretting in the middle of the night. He sees and controls the various moving pieces of your life. And he cares about you. He loves you to the point of letting his Son die as payment for your sins.

Take courage knowing the Almighty God absolutely loves you and is taking care of you even if life makes you feel otherwise. God will answer your prayers for his help. And he will guide you in the way you need to go.

*Lord, I'm humbled that you, who created
everything and oversee the universe,
are taking care of me, amen.*

October

"Give, and it will be given to you."

LUKE 6:38

Whenever you give, Jesus knows that you will receive far more in return. But receiving in kind—*I'll give for the sole reason that I'll get something back*—is not a Christlike motivation to give. God's design is about grace, about giving even when the recipient doesn't deserve it and can't repay it, about giving with no concern about the cost to yourself or about how your kindness might benefit you.

Still, something happens to us when we give to people in need in tangible, genuinely helpful ways. Consider what unique opportunities you have today to be a blessing to someone. You can pray for that friend who is sick. You can appreciate the clerk at the register. You can make an amazing meal for your friends. You yourself may not receive health, affirming words, or a feast because you do one of these things, but your heart will be fuller, and life will be richer.

Lord, please open my eyes to the needs of others today and free me to give generously, amen.

*Sluggards do not plow in season; so at
harvest time they look but find nothing.*

PROVERBS 20:4

*I*f you were asked to describe a godly person, would *industrious* be on your list?

Industriousness is actually an important trait of a godly person. When we choose to work hard, we glorify God by using the skills and abilities as well as the opportunity that he has given us. Our hard work will mean reaping a good harvest when the time comes, but it may also reap a harvest for God's kingdom. Why? Because when people ask why you work so hard, you may be able to explain that you are working to honor God. This perspective can compel us to work harder because we realize we are part of the bigger picture of shining God's light in this dark world.

Yes, preparing soil, planting seed, fertilizing, watering—all these tasks take time and call for industriousness. So we work hard and wait patiently for the harvest of souls that will come because God blessed our efforts in the workplace.

*Lord, I want to work hard at whatever
task you call me to, for the good of my
employer and for your glory, amen.*

Rejoice with those who rejoice;
mourn with those who mourn.

ROMANS 12:15

This simple guideline can have a profound impact on our everyday relationships as well as in our Christian community.

You sit next to a grieving friend, saying nothing, crying as she cries, just being there in the pain.

While mourning with those who mourn is not an easy assignment, the call to rejoice with people who rejoice may be more difficult. Whenever a friend succeeds at something or receives a huge blessing, we who are sinners by nature can react with envy. No wonder it's rare to see someone be genuinely joyful about another person's good news. To celebrate someone else's victory, though, is a beautiful and meaningful gift to that person.

Ask God to help you be the kind of friend who finds joy in someone else's joy and who grieves when another grieves. As you come alongside and share in your friend's sorrow and joy, you are doing more than obeying your King: you are making his love for her more real.

Lord, help me—today and every day—
to rejoice with those who rejoice and
mourn with those who mourn, amen.

"If you remain in me and my words remain in you, ask whatever you wish, and it will be done for you."

JOHN 15:7

What does it mean to "remain" or—as you'll find in other translations—"abide" in Jesus? In this context, the idea is to be deeply connected to Jesus and rooted in his love. We too easily focus on the promise in the latter part of John 15:7 without first recognizing the level of commitment Jesus calls for.

"Ask whatever you wish" is a reference to prayer, and the most effective prayer grows out of a genuine heart connection to Jesus. When we pray regularly, even continually, God works in our hearts, and we find our will lining up with his will for us. Clearly, prayer is a means of abiding.

Jesus also called his disciples to be sure that "my words remain in you." Bible study and Scripture memorization also join us to Jesus. Have we made it our aim to read his words and let them settle into our souls long enough that our actions joyfully follow?

Good things follow when we live close to Jesus.

Lord, teach me to abide in you, through prayer and your Word, amen.

God is our REFUGE & STRENGTH an ever-present HELP in trouble.

PSALM 46:1

*God is our refuge and strength, an
ever-present help in trouble.*

PSALM 46:1

Jesus spoke clearly: "In this world you will have trouble" (John 16:33). And all of us can attest to that truth. How much harder it would be, though, if we had to face every problem alone, without the help of our ever-present God, our refuge, and our strength.

First, God is our refuge: he is the best place to go when life careens out of control and a safe haven when people have hurt us. God shelters us, takes care of us, nurses our souls back to health, and protects us from further trouble.

Second, God is our strength. When we—who are made of dust—grow weak, he provides the energy and power we need to live a life that honors him. When we are mentally or emotionally spent, he again fills us with his strength.

Third, God is our ever-present help. He will always be with us, and he will always be helping us. Always.

What a friend you have in God! He loves you and longs to protect and help you.

*Lord, may I never hesitate to turn to you,
my refuge, strength, and help, amen.*

"From everyone who has been given much, much will be demanded; and from the one who has been entrusted with much, much more will be asked."

LUKE 12:48

Step by step, children grow in the amount of responsibility they can handle. So parents start by giving them little tasks—like picking up their toys. Soon the children can load the dishwasher or sweep the floor. Successfully shouldering these responsibilities is a building block for bigger jobs like mowing the lawn.

Similarly, we who are God's children move from smaller responsibilities to greater. God entrusts us with increasingly bigger tasks as we grow in our knowledge of him. And the more we grow spiritually, the greater the responsibilities we are ready for.

If you find yourself with more and more responsibility in the kingdom, rejoice. God is seeing your growth and rewarding you with responsibilities that will bless others and grow you even more.

Lord, thank you for growing my knowledge of you, deepening my relationship with you, entrusting me with greater responsibilities in your kingdom, and enabling me to fulfill them, amen.

IN QUIET-NESS & TRUST IS YOUR STRENGTH.
ISAIAH 30:15

"In quietness and trust is your strength."

ISAIAH 30:15

This truth comes from Isaiah, a prophet in the Old Testament, but it's a perfectly crafted reminder for us today.

Unfortunately, the world has a different perspective. It says that strength comes from voicing everything, in being louder than other voices. And trust? It's overrated, the world says, particularly when it's pointed toward God.

Don't let the world weaken your commitment to being with the Lord. Your right perspective on life in general as well as on specific situations will often come in the quiet moments you spend alone with God. When he isn't competing with the world's noise, you'll hear him more clearly. You'll also experience renewed strength when you choose to trust God instead of relying on your efforts.

Finally, God is trustworthy and kind, and you are his child who desperately needs his wise parental guidance. Trust, then, means letting him parent you throughout your day.

Lord, please help me find quiet places where I can listen for your voice—and then please help me to hear you, amen.

The LORD says, "During the forty years that I led you through the wilderness, your clothes did not wear out, nor did the sandals on your feet."

DEUTERONOMY 29:5

*I*n today's verse the Lord reminded Moses of his extravagant provision during the Israelites' forty-year wandering after they left Egypt. Constantly in the Old Testament, God encouraged the nation of Israel to remember his great faithfulness in guiding, protecting, and providing for them.

God called the people to look back because—like you and me—they were prone to forget about their faithful God's power and provision. Even immediately after the miraculous deliverance from Pharaoh and the amazing crossing of the Red Sea, the Israelites grumbled and panicked.

And we aren't very different from Israel. God longs for you to remember details of his faithfulness to you. When you do this, your trust muscle will grow. So take some time today to remember God's faithfulness to you and thank him for his kindness.

Lord, I am going to start right now to list the ways you have been faithful to me over the years. Use this list, I pray, to improve my memory and to help me to live with gratitude for your goodness, amen.

"Go into all the world and preach the gospel to all creation."

MARK 16:15

*B*efore ascending into heaven and before giving the Holy Spirit at Pentecost, the resurrected Jesus gave these instructions to the disciples. And imagine the fear the disciples must have felt as Jesus assigned them the impossible task of telling the entire world about him.

Thankfully, not long after Jesus spoke these words, the disciples received divine power. And when the Holy Spirit empowered the disciples, they couldn't help but share the gospel. It was a natural outflowing of their changed heart, Spirit-fueled passion, and Spirit-guided words.

Like the disciples may have felt, we may find it scary to share Jesus with others, but like the first disciples, we also have the Holy Spirit, who enables us to do the impossible. If you get nervous before talking to people about Jesus, simply ask the Spirit to give you the courage you need and the words the person needs to hear. He loves to answer that prayer because he loves to welcome people into his kingdom.

Lord, please show me one person today who needs the gospel—and then enable me to share it clearly, amen.

With God we will gain the victory, and
he will trample down our enemies.

PSALM 108:13

*N*otice that in writing this psalm, David didn't say that you will trample down your enemies. God will do that. Our natural desire is to pay back people who have caused us pain or dealt with us wrongly, but the consequences of their actions are for God to determine, not us.

The victory over the desire to seek and enact vengeance comes only when you are closely connected to God. When you are, you will find yourself releasing more and more of yourself and your life to him, letting him deal with your "enemies."

Don't live your life in bitterness. Choose the path of victory—the path of forgiving, letting go, and asking God to soften your wounded and hard heart. As you walk this path, pray for those who have injured you and trust that your loving God has you in the palm of his hand.

Lord, I trust you to bring justice in your time
and your way. And I ask you to help me forgive
the one(s) who hurt me so deeply, amen.

I CHRONICLES 4:10

Oh, that you would bless me and enlarge my territory! Let your hand be with me, and keep me from harm so that I will be free from pain.

1 CHRONICLES 4:10

An honorable man named Jabez prayed this powerful prayer. Having an attitude like his can greatly enhance your prayer life.

Ask God to *enlarge your territory* beyond your life of safety and ease. Ask him to stir you up and show you ministries to pursue that would take you out of your comfort zone. Ask him to unsettle you and lead you to walk in places where you absolutely have to trust him.

Ask that God's *hand would be with you.* Wherever you go, you need his hand of guidance and protection. You need his presence and power.

Ask God to *keep you from harm,* from the attack of the evil one, even from the harsh words of gossip and slander. This is not a prayer to escape the inevitability of heartache that comes in life. This is a prayer of surrender to the sovereign God, that he would have his way in your life.

Lord, enlarge my ministry. May your hand be with me. Please keep me from harm, amen.

*"Whoever does not carry their cross and
follow me cannot be my disciple."*

LUKE 14:27

What does it mean to carry your cross?

First of all, a literal cross was a brutal instrument of torture and death that destroyed anyone nailed to it. So to carry your cross is to completely die to yourself, to no longer be the same person.

So what—metaphorically speaking—is a cross we are to carry? When we die to what we want and instead follow God's will, we are carrying our cross. When we depend on God rather than strive for self-sufficiency, when we obey God rather than go our own way, when we follow Jesus and confess our faith in him no matter what doing so costs us, we are carrying our cross.

No matter what cross you bear today, remember this: Jesus carried his own cross, and he can empower you to carry yours.

*Lord, thank you that you will help me carry
my cross. I do need your help as you use my
cross to make me more like Jesus, amen.*

*Rebellion is like the sin of divination, and
arrogance like the evil of idolatry.*

1 SAMUEL 15:23

Divination and idolatry are heinous sins,
but here Samuel reminded us that
rebellion and arrogance are just as bad.

First, rebellion is having a heart contrary
to God. It is knowing what he wants us to do,
then actively going the other way, choosing
to disobey. It's devaluing what he values and
demeaning what he holds precious.

Second, arrogance is—simply put—pride.
You are convinced that your way is the only
way to live life, that your perspective is the only
way to look at a situation. Arrogant people
often make fun of others, actively promote
themselves, and even think they are smarter
than God!

The remedy for rebellion and arrogance is
viewing ourselves correctly. We are humans,
made of dust, finite and needy, sinful by
nature, in need of a Savior. When we humbly
acknowledge who we are in comparison to our
holy God, arrogance melts away, and rebellion
no longer seems wise.

*Lord, thank you that looking to you can free
me from rebellion and arrogance, amen.*

Do not conform to the pattern of this world, but
be transformed by the renewing of your mind.

ROMANS 12:2

You've heard of swimming like a fish in water? That's what we are: since we are swimming in the pattern of the world, we have a hard time discerning what it is. Put simply, it's the ungodly way of life the world advocates with its upside-down values and missing morals.

To be renewed in our minds—to fight this toxic environment—takes action and resolve. We choose to spend time with Jesus in prayer and Bible study. We make worshipping and spending time with fellow believers a priority. As we do these things, God works in our hearts to make us more like Jesus.

Instead of being greedy, for instance, we live with generosity. Instead of lying to get to the top, we tell the truth and entrust our professional path to the Lord. Instead of chasing after bodily perfection, we serve others in the body of Christ. And these are only a few examples of God's transformational work in our hearts!

Lord, renew my mind, transform my heart, and
use me as a light in this dark world, amen.

Unless the LORD builds the house,
the builders labor in vain.

PSALM 127:1

We spend a lot of time building our lives, don't we? Just living takes a lot of time. Sometimes we can get so caught up in the details of our lives that we can go days without connecting with God.

We are meant to live life in tandem with the Lord. He wants to guide and bless our steps. He longs to strengthen foundations of truth and love and joy. He desires to build into us traits like faithfulness, patience, and peace—traits that reflect his presence in our hearts and our lives.

Furthermore, no matter what you do, you cannot make yourself holy. You can't conjure up peace on your own. God is at work making you more holy, more like Jesus, and he blesses you with peace. And he wants to give you, his beloved child, so much more. So ask God to build you as he sees fit. Surrender to his direction and plans for you. He will build the house of your life, and it will be beautiful.

Lord, please build the house of my life.
I surrender to you today, amen.

*Because of the LORD's great love we are
not consumed, for his compassions
never fail. They are new every morning;
great is your faithfulness.*

LAMENTATIONS 3:22-23

This statement of faith comes in the midst of the struggling prophet's lamentations. What an example for us!

No matter what we are going through, we can take heart in the truths of these two verses. First, God greatly loves you. No matter what trials you're facing today, they will not swallow you up. People will fail you; your compassionate God will not. Ever. God's goodness toward us—his compassions—greet us every morning.

There's something else about a fresh, new morning. As the sun sets, we might be keenly aware of regrets, disappointments, and people's hurtful ways. Our tiredness at night can make all this overwhelming and every situation seem impossible.

But with the morning sun, you can find yourself rested, renewed, and feeling hopeful and encouraged. God may not change the circumstances, but with the sunrise he gives a fresh perspective on his power, love, and faithfulness.

*Lord, thank you for reminding me of your
faithfulness with every sunrise, amen.*

Love the LORD your God with all your heart and
with all your soul and with all your strength.

DEUTERONOMY 6:5

We are to love God with all that we are, with all of our will, all of our minds, all of our emotions, and all of our physical power. We are to bow the knee and our heart to the King of kings and hold back nothing when we worship him.

David worshipped like that. Aptly called a man after God's own heart, he lavishly loved God. Yes, David sometimes strayed terribly and sinned greatly. Still, he loved his God.

Similarly, Peter promised he'd never forsake the Lord, but not long after, he denied even knowing Jesus. Still, he chose to return to Jesus and follow him.

And all of us are like David and Peter. All of us have the opportunity to continuously love God. And all of us get off track. We'll disappoint our Lord when we choose to sin. But because he is gracious, we can always be once again people after God's own heart.

Don't let your personal failures and shame prevent you from loving God with all you are.

Lord, teach me to love you faithfully
and with all that I am, amen.

The LORD detests all the proud of heart. Be sure of this: They will not go unpunished.

PROVERBS 16:5

*L*ook around. The world rewards the proud, doesn't it? People who believe they can do anything, who boast about their abilities, and who never admit fault often "make it" in the world. They climb corporate ladders, scale the heights of sports achievement, and scrap their way to fame.

Of course, not all successful and famous people are proud, nor are humble people immune to pride. Insidious pride can affect us all. When we declare, "I can live my life in my own strength. I don't need God," that's pride. When we turn our backs on God and go our own ways, that's pride. And God "detests all the proud of heart."

But God is pleased and honored by those who humbly accept his leadership and receive his strength into their lives. So choose each day—and several times throughout each day—to humble yourself and depend solely on him.

Lord, I don't want to be prideful and full of myself. I want to be humble and full of you, amen.

The battle is not yours, but God's.
2 chronicles 20:15

This is what the Lord says to you: "Do not be afraid or discouraged because of this vast army. For the battle is not yours, but God's."

2 CHRONICLES 20:15

These are Jahaziel's words to King Jehoshaphat when he faced the armies of Moab and Ammon, and the king responded by bowing before God and worshipping him. The next morning when they set out, Jehoshaphat appointed certain men to sing the praises of God. And as they praised the Lord, he delivered Israel from their enemies. The battle—the victory—was indeed God's.

What battle are you facing today? Unless you've chosen a battle you have no business entering, these words are for you too. You may feel like you are up against something stronger than you are. Even so, be strong. Encourage yourself with the truth that this is not your battle; it is the Lord's.

Choose today to be like Jehoshaphat's army and sing praises to God. Tell him how great he is. You'll find your worries fading as you sing to your faithful, powerful God, reminding yourself of all the victories he has brought in your life.

Lord, instead of worrying, I'm choosing to sing to you and worship you, amen.

To him who is able to keep you from stumbling
and to present you before his glorious
presence without fault and with great joy .
. . be glory, majesty, power and authority.

JUDE VV. 24–25

Jude poured a lot of solid theology and godly wisdom into these thirty words!

First, God is "able to keep you from stumbling," from tripping on erroneous teaching and falling into sin and away from your faith in Jesus. God does this through his Holy Spirit, who lives within you as Teacher, Guide, and Helper. The Spirit is with you no matter what temptation you face, whatever decisions you need to make, and whatever paths you need to choose from.

Second, Jude also taught that God will usher you into the presence of his glory, where you will praise him for eternity just as Jude praised him in these two verses. Jesus' saving work on the cross—his work of love—understandably prompts our worship and great joy.

Lord, thank you for the salvation you
provided through Jesus Christ and the
gift of the Spirit that I may honor you
with my life. I'm grateful, amen.

*"From the least to the greatest,
all are greedy for gain."*

JEREMIAH 6:13

On behalf of God, Jeremiah, the weeping prophet, spoke these words about and to the nation of Israel, but his words are still true today. Too many of us aren't satisfied with what we have. Instead we long for the next thing, then the next.

Such greed is the opposite of God's generosity. So when we live lives of greed, we don't please God or accurately represent him. The nation of Israel was to be a light on the hill, shining forth God's goodness. But they failed: they were too busy in their pursuit of more and more.

When "all are greedy for gain," all of us lose. If instead we chose to live outrageously generous lives, all of us would win. God's people giving and receiving, glorifying him by their obedience and love, could truly be a light in this dark world, declaring with our actions the goodness of God.

Lord, forgive me when I've not been satisfied with what you've given me, when I want more stuff rather than wanting more of you, amen.

Though I walk in the midst of
trouble, you preserve my life.

PSALM 138:7

*N*one of us likes to walk through trouble and pain. We'd rather avoid feeling relational stress, fretting about finances, aching for a prodigal's return, grieving the loss of a spouse through death or divorce, exhausted to the point of discouragement by an over-busy life. But in God's kingdom economy, we grow best through adversity.

The psalmist understood this truth, acknowledging both the inevitability of trouble in our lives and the unshakeable faithfulness of God. We will walk in the midst of trouble, if not today, then tomorrow. Life has a way of pummeling us—but, according to today's verse, God has a way of preserving us. In the midst of trials, he will preserve our lives.

Now, preserving you doesn't necessarily mean delivering you from the trials that arise. What preserving does mean is that God walks through the troubles with you. You will indeed know his presence with you—his love, vitality, hope, and joy—in the midst of your pain.

Lord, thank you that you preserve me and
walk with me through my troubles, amen.

*Blessed is the one who does not walk in step
with the wicked or stand in the way that
sinners take or sit in the company of mockers.*

PSALM 1:1

The psalmist warned us: don't walk, stand, or sit with the wrong people.

We are not to *walk* the way the wicked walk. We are not to conform to the world's selfish ways and upside-down values. We're not to chase after success at the expense of others. Instead, we are to walk the path of righteousness God has established for his people.

We are not to *stand* in the road where sinners walk. We are not to hang out with people who live in rebellion against God. If we do, our love for him can slip as we gradually move from loving him to wanting to impress others.

We are not to *sit* with people who mock the Lord, his church, and our faith. Mocking of public figures is well accepted in our culture, and social media offers opportunities for judgment, self-righteousness, and, yes, mocking.

In contrast to these three behaviors, may our lives reflect our walk with Jesus.

*Lord, I want to walk in your footsteps, stand
in your pathway, and sit with you, amen.*

Blessed
Le
IS THE
ONE who
does NOT
walk
IN
STEP
with the
Wicked.
Le

PSALM 1:1

*Who will not fear you, Lord, and bring glory
to your name? For you alone are holy.*

REVELATION 15:4

*A*t the end of the age—when King Jesus
returns—every knee will bow before
him, and everyone will recognize him as
Lord. His glory will fill the new heavens and
the new earth. There, freed from sin, clothed
in the righteousness of Christ, having new
resurrection bodies, and filled with awe and
gratitude, we will perfectly glorify God. We will
undoubtedly find ourselves worshipping him
as naturally as we breathe.

And of course we aren't waiting until
then to worship God. What can you do to get
a glimpse of God's beauty and glory today?
When will you take time today to think about
all that he has done for you and thank him?
What can help you be more concerned about
his opinion of you than you are about other
people's?

Take some time right now to worship God
and praise him for who he is. Oh, how good he
is to you! Oh, how much he loves you!

*Lord, may I live a life of worship here on
earth as I will one day in heaven, amen.*

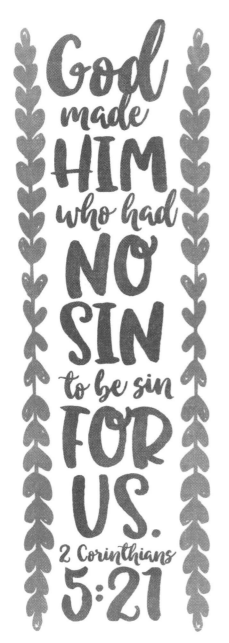

*God made him who had no sin to be
sin for us, so that in him we might
become the righteousness of God.*

2 CORINTHIANS 5:21

This verse powerfully summarizes the gospel with elegant simplicity.

Jesus—God's beautiful Son—was without sin. Yet he became our sin on the cross. In Jesus, God condemned all sins for all time. With his broken body and shed blood, Jesus satisfied God's justice, then ushered all sinners before God's throne. We are no longer known as sinners, but as righteous ones—all because of Jesus' amazing sacrifice.

Your salvation from the punishment for your sins is not up to you—and you couldn't save yourself if you had to. But you don't have to save yourself. You've been saved: the price has been paid once and for all.

Living in light of this grace is freeing. You no longer have to look over your shoulder, worrying if you "made it" into God's kingdom. Again, your salvation is not dependent on you; it's dependent on Jesus' perfect sacrifice on the cross. Thank him for that today.

*Lord, I'm grateful for your sacrifice. Thank
you that I can walk in freedom today,
knowing my salvation is sure in you, amen.*

Caleb silenced the people before Moses and said, "We should go up and take possession of the land, for we can certainly do it."

NUMBERS 13:30

Of course Caleb saw the giants. He and Joshua saw the threat as clearly as the other ten spies did. The difference was, both Joshua and Caleb knew God was greater than the enemy. They knew the enemy was mighty—and they knew God was mightier.

Both groups saw the same giants, but each group interpreted the situation differently— one looked through eyes of faith, and the other, through eyes of fear. Their idea about what Israel should do was based on their perspective.

You have that same choice today. Will you focus on the gigantic circumstances that are overwhelming you, or will you settle your soul by remembering God's faithfulness to you and believing he will prevail? With faith in God, you can live with confidence like Caleb did. You'll see beyond the current struggle. You'll be looking to your good and powerful God and trusting him to deliver you. The choice is yours.

Lord, I praise you for being bigger than my giants and able to deliver me. Thank you in advance for rescuing me, amen.

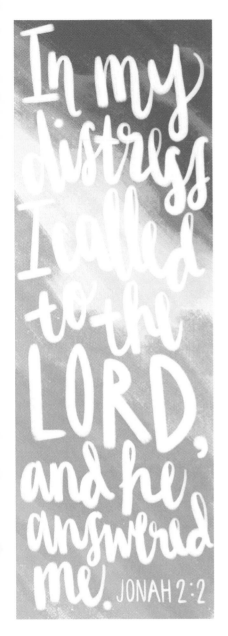

In my distress I called to the
LORD, and he answered me.

JONAH 2:2

*Y*ou may know the story. Jonah called on the Lord from the belly of a gigantic fish. Jonah was there because he had rebelled against God when the Almighty told him to preach to the evil Ninevites. Jonah had responded by jumping on a boat and going the opposite direction.

Yet God rescued Jonah; he responded when Jonah called out to him from his deepest distress. And Jonah's experience offers good news for us. Why? Because we don't have to have everything together to be able to call on God for help and rescue.

The bottom line is, God responds to our cries of desperation. Yes, we sin. We are human, often broken, and too often stubborn. But the moment we realize our need for God's intervention—the moment we choose to reach out to him from the pit we've chosen, if not created, for ourselves—is the moment God answers our call, rescues us, and gives us a second chance to obey him and please him.

Lord, I thank you that I don't have
to have my life or my heart in order
before I can call on you, amen.

"Whatever you ask for in prayer, believe that you have received it, and it will be yours."

MARK 11:24

Jesus told this amazing truth to his disciples, encouraging them to have a solid belief in his ability to answer prayer. So what is going on when we pray for something for years without seeing an answer? Is this verse not true? Or is our faith not strong enough?

To understand not-yet-answered prayer, it's important to look at the whole counsel of Scripture. For instance, in the Lord's Prayer, we read that we are to pray for God's kingdom to come on earth, for our King's will to be done on earth just as it is done in heaven.

This kind of praying is different from giving Jesus a laundry list of wants. Instead, we share our hearts, but we defer to his will. We also ask him to work in our hearts so that our prayers come to reflect his desires.

Remember, too, that God answers prayers with "no" and "wait" as well as the "yes" we hope for.

Lord, I know you may not answer my prayer my way. Even so, help me to have patience and faith in your good and loving ways, amen.

Create in me a pure heart, O God, and renew a steadfast spirit within me.

PSALM 51:10

David cried out to God in desperation. The king had committed the sin of adultery and tried to cover it up with the sin of murder. Only after God sent Nathan the prophet to confront him did David more fully realize the magnitude of his sin and pray the words of today's verse.

David's prayer is a good model for us when we go before God to confess the ways we have sinned and willfully gone our own way. First, we ask God to scrub our hearts clean, for we cannot clean ourselves. Only God can forgive our sins. Only God can make us clean.

In the aftermath of our sin, we are well aware of our weakness and the ease with which we can fall into sin. That's why it's important to ask that God give us a steadfast spirit, a desire to faithfully follow him no matter what.

So, no matter how far you've strayed, turn to God for forgiveness and cleansing. He will give you a fresh start.

Lord, I do desire a clean heart and a steadfast spirit. Please bless me with both, amen.

Create in Me a pure Heart O God.

PSALM 51:10

What does the LORD require of you?
To act justly and to love mercy and
to walk humbly with your God.

MICAH 6:8

Obedience to these three requirements means putting love into action.

To act justly may be inconvenient. To show mercy may mean helping those who can't repay you. To walk humbly with God is to do what he calls us to do—to bow before him, listen to his voice, and surrender our wills to his. Love in action can mean counseling unwed moms, watching a single parent's children for a weekend, or visiting lonely people in assisted-living facilities.

And you can love this way because the One who commands is—according to today's Scripture—"your God." As your Creator, he knows what you are able to do. As your heavenly Father, he wants you to do as he asks. As your sovereign King, he will enable you to obey. And in this case, your God will help you love.

Lord, thank you for loving me well and
helping me love others well, amen.

YOU ARE ALREADY CLEAN BECAUSE OF THE WORD I HAVE SPOKEN TO YOU

JOHN 15:3

"You are already clean because of the word I have spoken to you."

JOHN 15:3

Kids teach parents a lot of things. One thing is just how dirty, dirty can be. A trip to the sandbox means sand everywhere: in the pockets of the jeans, in the shoes, and under fingernails. Getting a squirming toddler clean is work!

In John 15, Jesus addressed the matter of spiritual cleanness. He spoke these life-giving words to the disciples, fully knowing that one man's uncleanness would soon prompt a betrayal that would lead to Jesus' arrest and crucifixion. Still, he invited all twelve of the disciples to be washed.

What they didn't know was that cleanliness of spirit would come at a high price: Jesus' own blood would soon be spilled, and that blood was key to forgiveness and clean hearts. Jesus' blood welcomes us all to him despite the fact that we're like sandy toddlers. We now can be baptized and have clean hearts because of what he did.

Let's not be toddlers who fight the suds. Instead, may we welcome the spiritual cleansing that Jesus made possible.

Lord, thank you for making a way for me to be cleaned, inside and out, amen.

November

Let us not become conceited, provoking and envying each other.

GALATIANS 5:26

To be conceited is to be smug about your abilities and accomplishments, pridefully ignoring the fact that God gave you those abilities and enabled all your accomplishments.

Paul warned the Galatians that such conceit can lead to other bad behavior that hurts other people and, inevitably, hurts us.

For instance, when we are self-centered and pleased with ourselves, we can see others as rivals and even as threats to our happiness. Often that perspective prompts us to provoke others and put them down in order to make ourselves feel better.

Conceit can also make us give in to the green monster of envy. Rather than choosing satisfaction and contentment with what God has given us, we allow ourselves to be too aware of what others have. Our joy evaporates because that person has more of something we want.

The opposite of conceit is humility, a Christlike trait that enables us to serve others, live at peace with people, and be happy with our friends' blessings.

Lord, I'm so grateful for you and for this warning. Work in my heart and help me to choose humility over conceit today, amen.

"Abba, Father," he said, "everything is possible for you. Take this cup from me. Yet not what I will, but what you will."

MARK 14:36

In this intimate snapshot of his agonizing prayer, Jesus called the Almighty God "Daddy" (*Abba*).

Looming before Jesus was the cross—an instrument of torture and death. Even darker was the pall of the sin he would bear. That sin would weigh down his sinless soul and—for the first time in eternity past—separate him from his *Abba*.

So of course Jesus asked Daddy to deliver him.

But Daddy was silent. This sacrificial death of his only Son was essential to his plan to rescue humanity from the grips of sin, Satan, and death. The Son must fulfill his mission.

Jesus sweated drops of blood as he continued to pray and beg for a different solution. He knew the cup that awaited would bring unimaginable pain—physical, emotional, and spiritual. Yet Jesus chose obedience. He chose his Daddy's will, not his human will. And because Jesus did that, you can live in relationship with your heavenly Daddy.

Lord, thank you. Thank you for your truly amazing grace, amen.

*"No one can see the kingdom of God
unless they are born again."*

JOHN 3:3

*N*icodemus was a respected Pharisee, an expert in Jewish law, "a member of the Jewish ruling council," and that is why he approached Jesus in the shadow of night with his questions about salvation. Jesus responded with today's verse about being born again. It's hard to imagine how perplexing Nicodemus found these words.

The question he asked reveals how puzzled he was: "How can someone be born when they are old? . . . Surely they cannot enter a second time into their mother's womb to be born!" (3:4). Nicodemus heard Jesus' words literally.

But Jesus was saying that to be saved, we have to undergo a radical transformation, one so complete that it's as if we have been given a new heart for a brand-new approach to life. We can't make this happen. Only by committing ourselves to Christ—only by following his pattern of death (dying to our self, our wishes, our control of our life), then resurrection (surrendering our life to Jesus) can we be born again.

*Lord, thank you for choosing me to be born
again into your eternal kingdom, amen.*

*Jesus told [Thomas], "Because you have
seen me, you have believed; blessed are those
who have not seen and yet have believed."*

JOHN 20:29

*L*ook again at Jesus' words. He was speaking about you—he was commending you—in the second part of this verse. Thomas had the advantage of meeting Jesus in the flesh, and Thomas believed because he saw the resurrected Lord. Yet you believe even though you haven't seen Jesus. And you believe that God sent Jesus from heaven to our dark and fallen earth to live a perfect, sinless life. The spotless Lamb of God, Jesus satisfied the requirements of a sin sacrifice: he died on the cross for every sin ever committed—past, present, and future. Jesus' death opened the door for all of us to be redeemed, but his death is not the end of his story or ours. His resurrection proved that he was the long-awaited Messiah.

Do you believe? If so, know that Jesus spoke blessings over individuals like you who believe without seeing him with your eyes.

*Lord, I thank you for the grace you pour into my
life, specifically for giving me faith in you, amen.*

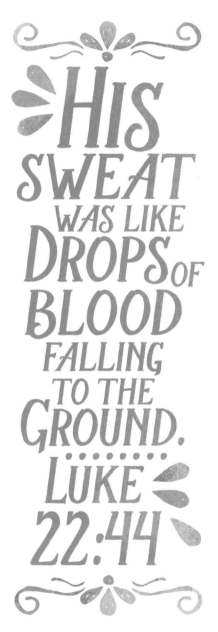

HIS SWEAT WAS LIKE DROPS OF BLOOD FALLING TO THE GROUND. LUKE 22:44

Being in anguish, [Jesus] prayed more earnestly, and his sweat was like drops of blood falling to the ground.

LUKE 22:44

Here we see that Jesus shed his blood for us even before he was nailed to the cross. Notice what caused Jesus' bleeding: he revealed his anguish as he carried out the Father's plan, which meant excruciating suffering and carrying the weight of every sin upon himself.

Because of his love for the human beings God and he had crafted, Jesus chose to suffer. He yielded his will to the will of the Father, let himself be crucified, and then rose from the dead. And now, seated at the right hand of God, the resurrected Jesus prays for you who love him!

Lord, I'm humbled that you chose pain and suffering for my sake, amen.

November 6

"Ask where the good way is, and walk in it, and you will find rest for your souls."

JEREMIAH 6:16

Think about God's commands for a minute. Every single one of them is for our own good, isn't it? So is this call to walk in the good way wherever God directs, and the promised good result is rest for your soul.

What is "the good way"? God has answered this question in his Word. The good way is to live a life characterized by love, service, obedience to God, and trust in him. Where is that good way for you specifically? It is wherever God shows you, guides you, places you.

As you walk where God wants you to walk and as you walk in the way God wants you to walk, you will know the peace that comes with obedience, you will know the blessing of your heavenly Father's pleasure in you, and you will know rest for your soul.

Lord, please show me where you would have me walk and then, I ask, enable me to walk in such a way that points people to you, amen.

Therefore, my dear friends, flee from idolatry.

1 CORINTHIANS 10:14

Living in idolatry means living for lesser gods than the one true God of the Bible. A lesser god is anything that is not God, anything that takes your affection and attention away from him.

We worship anything but God. Wealth, fame, possessions, the American Dream, relationships, youth, perfect health, physical appearance—any and all of these can too easily push God from his rightful place of prominence in our lives.

So how do we flee from idolatry? By worshipping Someone greater than what we have made an idol. By stopping the treadmill of life, ceasing to pursue success at any cost and thereby giving ourselves space to worship God alone. By listing God's attributes and praising him for all those and more, for being kind, holy, loving, wise, beautiful, powerful, and strong. By remembering his faithfulness, bowing down before him, and singing songs of adoration.

You have the opportunity today to turn away from idols once and for all and to wholeheartedly commit to following after God. Oh, how he loves you and longs for your full devotion!

Lord, I choose to worship you
and you alone, amen.

I will instruct you and teach you in the way you should go; I will counsel you with my loving eye on you.

PSALM 32:8

*A*re you someone who wants to know what's next in life? Many of us don't like living with question marks; we crave certainty; we'd love to know where God is taking us. This verse promises that God will lead us, it promises his counsel and love, but it doesn't give us an itinerary.

Knowing the path God has for your life comes only with being in relationship with him. Saying, "I will," God promises to teach us and counsel us in the way we should go, and he will lovingly keep his eye on us to keep us walking in the right direction.

If you're confused about what's next in your life, if you desperately need to know what to do, listen for God's instruction. That may mean prayer, journaling, a time of waiting, and/or counsel from those who know you and know God.

Remember, though, that God says, "I will."

Lord, thank you that you want to tell me where you want me, that I don't have to guess. Please help me hear you and obey, amen.

He is my
Refuge
and my
Fortress,
my God,
in whom
I trust.

PSALM 91:2

*He is my refuge and my fortress,
my God, in whom I trust.*

PSALM 91:2

In Jesus, God came to earth to rescue us from our sin nature and the consequences of the sin we commit. He wants to eradicate our sin because he longs to have a relationship with us. He wants us to declare—like the psalmist—that he is "my God." That possessive *my* reveals a relationship, trust, and intimacy. And this is available to you.

God is completely trustworthy and the best Friend you'll ever have. He keeps his promises. He will never leave you. He isn't put off by your struggles. He forgives sin, removing it as far from you as the east is from the west (Psalm 103:12). And he loves with unconditional love.

Furthermore, God wants to protect his people from harm. He offers his children an escape from worries, troubles, and strife, a place to rest, a refuge. And that refuge is at the same time a fortress where his children find safety and security.

*Lord, my refuge, my fortress, my
trustworthy God, I love you, amen.*

*"It is not the healthy who need a
doctor, but the sick. I have not come
to call the righteous, but sinners."*

MARK 2:17

Jesus didn't come for people who appeared to have their lives all together. He didn't come for the smugly religious, the self-sufficient, or the proud. Jesus came to save sinners—which is everyone. But in this context, Jesus came to save those of us who recognize that we are sinners from our sin and its consequences.

As you've probably noticed, though, not everyone wants to be saved; not everyone feels a need to be saved. When we tell people about Jesus, it's often much easier when they understand that without him they are sick and needy, when they already recognize their sinfulness and their need for a Savior. Comfortable, self-sufficient people don't listen in the same way—and we can't convince them that they actually need God.

When God brings people into your life who are hurting, who know they need healing, offer wise counsel, genuine friendship, a listening ear, and especially the wonderful truth about Jesus' love.

*Lord, please bring into my life people who
need to know Jesus' forgiveness and love—
and then speak through me, amen.*

*But the Lord God called to the
man, "Where are you?"*

GENESIS 3:9

*A*dam and Eve had chosen to eat from
the tree God had forbidden. Soon after
their disobedience, God called, "Where are
you?" The all-knowing God wasn't stumped.

No, the holy God knew exactly where now-
sinful Adam and Eve were—cowering, hiding
in the bushes, desperately trying to cover their
nakedness. So why did God ask this question?
Because God wants relationship with us even
though we sin.

It had been the habit of Adam and Eve to
spend time with the Lord in the cool of the eve-
nings. So when God stood where they usually
met and the couple wasn't there, God asked a
question that revealed his desire for relationship: Where are you? Why aren't you here?

God intended to woo them back into
relationship. He asked a question because he
wanted a response, and Adam responded. God
heard the details; we hear God's cursing of the
serpent, the woman, and the man; and then we
see the Lord's grace. He sacrificed an animal to
cover their shame. In the future he would sacrifice his beloved Son to cover your sin and mine.

*Lord, thank you for wanting to be in
relationship with sinful me, amen.*

But the
LORD
God
CALLED
to the
MAN,

Where
are
you?

GENESIS 3:9

"I tell you that you are Peter, and on this rock I will build my church, and the gates of Hades will not overcome it."

MATTHEW 16:18

You are the Christ, the Son of the living God." That was Peter's bold statement that prompted Jesus' words above. Many scholars understand Jesus to mean that this truth about himself being God's Son, Messiah, and Lord would be the foundation of believers collectively being the church but also individually.

Is your life built on the idea of Jesus' lordship? Recognizing Jesus as your Savior is not the same as naming him your Lord. When we acknowledge our sins, confess them, and choose to believe that Jesus was the perfect sacrifice who paid the penalty for them, we accept him as our Savior.

To live with Jesus as our Lord, though, means following him every single day, asking what he wants for our lives, and obeying him. Already secure in our relationship with him, we now demonstrate our gratitude by surrendering to his will for our lives. *That* is building our lives on a rock-solid foundation.

Lord, I praise you, my Savior. Help me to live with you as my Lord, amen.

FAITH IS CONFI-DENCE IN WHAT WE HOPE FOR. Hebrews 11:1

Faith is confidence in what we hope for and assurance about what we do not see.

HEBREWS 11:1

It's easy to have faith when everything is going smoothly. It's another thing, however, to have faith when we can't see around the bend in the road of life. Having faith means having a different sort of vision—the ability to see God's work even when we cannot see his hand.

God often brings difficult circumstances into our lives to help us build our faith muscle. When bills are due and there's no money to pay them, either we can give in to panic, or we can exercise that faith muscle, believing that our heavenly Father knows our need and can supernaturally provide. This doesn't mean the check will always come in the mail. When the check doesn't show up, God then provides us with the ability to endure hardship.

And the presence of hardship doesn't negate God's love for you. In fact, because he loves you, he loves to build your faith. Your job is simply to choose to have faith in him, no matter what you see around you.

Lord, I want a stronger faith muscle. Please give me strength for today's workout, amen.

November 14

In their hearts humans plan their course,
but the LORD establishes their steps.

PROVERBS 16:9

We use the brains God gave us to figure out the best course of action for enriching our relationships, furthering our careers, and benefitting our families. But sometimes, even with our most prayerful planning and the wisest of counsel, we find out that our plans aren't the same as God's, as the several holy redirects he does along the way indicate!

Why does God redirect us? Because he loves us. He actually shows us his love and his kindness by changing our path and then establishing our steps. He helps us to see our wrong thinking and teaches us to make kingdom choices instead of selfish ones. And, as the Author of history, God oversees its unfolding and even allows us to participate in his redemption of the human race.

Back to the plans you make. Have you ever realized you were walking down the wrong route? Don't worry, because nothing you do can mess up God's ultimate plan.

Lord, thank you that—in your infinite
wisdom and love—you guide my steps
according to your good plans for me, amen.

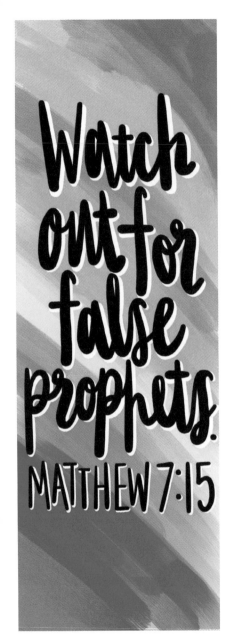

"Watch out for false prophets. They come to you in sheep's clothing, but inwardly they are ferocious wolves."

MATTHEW 7:15

Jesus warned the disciples about people who say they are representing God, but who are not speaking truth. These deceivers pretend to be Christians. Their words seem acceptable at first hearing, but their message is inevitably recognized as being contrary to the gospel.

The aim of these wolves is to lure people away from Jesus, from the cross, and from his call to discipleship—and that is bait for spiritual death. These false teachers may deny the resurrection, or they may try to persuade people that they have to do more than trust in Jesus if they want to be saved.

The best way to deal with false teachers is to know God's truth so well that you easily spot a fake. It's to reorient yourself to the truth of the gospel. Know the truth—and practice explaining it in case God gives you the opportunity to protect others from the world's false prophets.

Lord, may I never fail to marvel at the gospel truth—or to share it when you give me the opportunity. Keep me alert! Amen.

[The people at the temple] recognized him as the same man who used to sit begging at the temple gate called Beautiful, and they were filled with wonder and amazement at what had happened to him.

ACTS 3:10

*P*eter and John did not have silver or gold when the lame beggar asked them for money, but they had Jesus Christ. And in that moment of holy connection, they offered Jesus to this man. He asked for temporary relief, but they gave him a lifetime of walking. His response was to walk and jump—praising God for legs that worked! As a result, many came to know this powerful Jesus. People were amazed and wanted to know how this amazing miracle happened.

If you are a Christ follower, do you realize that a similar miracle has happened to you? When you encountered Jesus, you were lame of soul. But Jesus didn't leave you lying in your hopelessness. He set you on your feet and blessed you with peace and joy. Like this once-lame man, you have great reasons to praise God!

Lord, may I respond to your work in my life by walking and jumping—praising you for my revitalized soul! Amen.

Be quick to listen, slow to speak & slow to become Angry. James 1:19

Everyone should be quick to listen, slow
to speak and slow to become angry,
because human anger does not produce
the righteousness that God desires.

JAMES 1:19-20

*O*h, if only we could do what James said here. How many times have we failed to listen to the hearts of our loved ones? How many times have we reacted with anger rather than patience?

As James reminded us here, our anger gets in the way of living a righteous and God-glorifying life. Thankfully, even when we unleash unkind words, God offers abundant grace when we go to him in confession. Then we can choose to go to the one we spoke to angrily and say the most beautiful seven words—*I was wrong. Will you forgive me?* Today you have a choice. You can be either quick to listen and slow to anger or slow to listen and quick to anger. When someone tries your patience, take a deep breath and ask God to help you listen and let go of anger.

Lord, I want to be a blessing to people
I know, so please help me listen rather
than react with anger, amen.

The LORD is compassionate and gracious,
slow to anger, abounding in love.

PSALM 103:8

How could we not love, follow, and serve such a God!

May we love him by extending to others the kind of compassion and grace, patience and love that he extends to us! And may we treat ourselves with those life-giving traits as well.

First, though, how well are you reflecting God on these four points? Whom are you blessing with compassion and grace? With patience? With love? Or whom could you be blessing? Ask God not only to show you but also to empower you.

Second, how well are you treating yourself? God is compassionate and gracious toward us, but we can be ruthless to ourselves. We might show others compassion, but we criticize ourselves: *You should have known better. You'll never overcome this. You're stupid.* We are unkind and angry with ourselves, impatient and unloving. Yet Jesus has commanded us to love our neighbors as we love ourselves. Are your neighbors in trouble?

Lord, teach me to be kind, compassionate,
gracious, patient, and loving to myself so
that I may better love others, amen.

It is God who arms me with strength and keeps my way secure.

2 Samuel 22:33

*It is God who arms me with strength
and keeps my way secure.*

2 SAMUEL 22:33

You can live life with strength and security! You might feel you've got to muster up strength to impress God, to prove your worth. You might see weakness as failure, but the opposite is true. He arms you with strength when you realize you can't do life without him. As you surrender, you put yourself in the perfect position to receive strength and security from God.

When our security is grounded on something removable, we tend to crash when the unexpected happens. Job loss plunges us into fear's pit. A broken friendship makes us never want to risk again. An unexpected disease rattles our confidence in the future.

Overwhelming trials may have you feeling weak. Tragedy might have shattered your sense of security. But rest today in knowing that Jesus is here for you. He will gladly give you the strength and security you long for. All you have to do is ask.

Lord, help me to recognize my need for your strength and to seek the security I can find only in you. Oh, how I need you today! Amen.

"I know the plans I have for you," declares the
LORD, "plans to prosper you and not to harm
you, plans to give you hope and a future."

JEREMIAH 29:11

When we look at this well-known verse, we find reassurance that God is in control of our lives and has good things for us. But this promise is much more far-reaching.

First, consider the context. Jeremiah was speaking God's words to encourage the nation of Israel, who had been exiled to Babylon. Many people who first heard these words wouldn't experience deliverance from Babylon. Instead, they would continue to learn to thrive in a place that was hard, buoyed by hope for their children.

Now consider this promise's even bigger span. Ultimately, God will bring his people out of this earth where we are foreigners and into his heavenly kingdom. The hope we have is Jesus' return; the future will be life in a new earth under a new heaven.

So these words offer hope to us as individuals just as they offered hope to the people of Israel and just as they offer hope to Christ followers today, for he *will* reign forever!

Lord, thank you for your promises and
your promised future reign, amen.

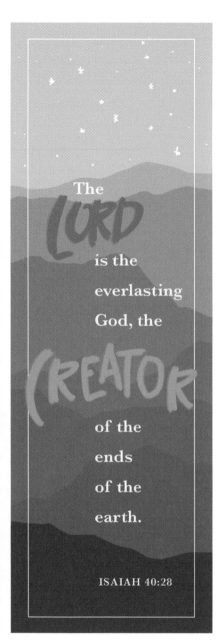

The LORD is the everlasting God, the Creator of the ends of the earth. He will not grow tired or weary, and his understanding no one can fathom.

ISAIAH 40:28

*I*n this busy world, we see many exhausted and work-weary people. We get tired out by life's seemingly impossible demands and the pressure to meet them. After all, we are human beings with a finite amount of energy and limited abilities. Every night we must sleep to renew our energy level. We need to eat to regain our strength. We must exercise to stay strong.

But God does not have such limitations. He doesn't need food or sleep to keep going. His strength will never fade, and his understanding is all-encompassing and thorough. Simply put, he knows everything about everything.

And this God is with you every day of your life, 24/7. He is there when you grow weary, hungry, weak, or overwhelmed, offering you his unlimited strength. And he calls you to a relationship with him, a relationship that will give you perspective, wisdom, soul rest, grace, hope, and joy in your busy life.

Lord, I need your power today to power through my day, amen.

*Trust in the Lord with all your heart and
lean not on your own understanding;
in all your ways submit to him, and
he will make your paths straight.*

PROVERBS 3:5-6

To trust in God means to stop trying to understand every aspect of life and do everything in your own strength. After all, we human beings simply don't understand everything. We don't even understand our own hearts, much less another person's heart or the world's inner workings. Next to God, we actually know very little. It's crazy to try to do life on our own.

So it's important to trust that God is sovereign and good, that he loves us and knows what is best for us, and that he can run the universe quite smoothly without our help. This proverb also instructs us to "submit to him," and that letting go of our will and accepting his will for us is trust in action. When we surrender our lives to him, we can know his peace.

When you choose to depend on Jesus, he will make your paths straight. Will you surrender—or recommit—your life to him right now?

*Lord, I want to live in dependence
on you who love me, amen.*

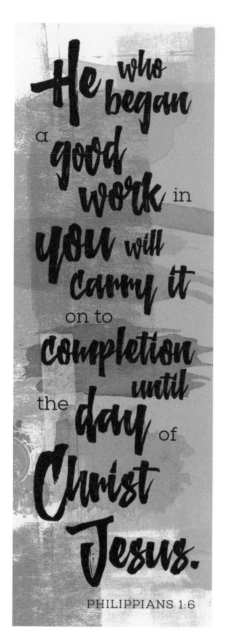

PHILIPPIANS 1:6

He who began a good work in you will carry it on to completion until the day of Christ Jesus.

PHILIPPIANS 1:6

Have you ever been discouraged about your growth as a Christian—or its apparent absence? All of us stumble. When we stand back up, we may take three steps back. We lurch ahead, only to fall flat. We long to do the right thing, but too often we don't act.

Hear the good news Paul shared above. God had begun doing a good work in the Philippian church, and he promised to complete what he had started.

Let the truth that God finishes what he starts encourage you today. The moment you met him, he began the work of making you more like Jesus. He started softening your heart toward him and others. He began to teach you patience, endurance, and how to find joy in painful circumstances. He sparked and enriched your prayer life.

You may feel like you're constantly struggling, but believe God's Word: the Holy Spirit within you is working in you to make you more like Jesus every single day. And he will complete that very good work.

Lord, show me how you're continuing the work you've begun in me, amen.

*The LORD God is a sun and shield; the LORD
bestows favor and honor; no good thing does he
withhold from those whose walk is blameless.*

PSALM 84:11

ook at some of the blessings our gracious
God adds to lives of his obedient children as we live, blameless, in Jesus.

First, God is our sun who, like the sun of our
solar system, provides warmth, sustenance,
and light. Without the sun, the world would
freeze, and no living thing would survive. Sun
is essential to the growth of food, and the sun's
light enables life as we know it. Similarly, God
provides his people with the warmth of his
love, the sustenance of his truth, and the light
of his presence with us.

Second, God is like a shield that protects
a soldier from an attacking enemy's sword. In
the same way, God shields us from the fiery
darts of the evil one, from gossip and slander,
from the world's untruth and darkness.

What blessings! God shines on you today,
giving light and life, and he will be your shield
of protection.

*Lord, I praise you for being my Sun
and my Shield as well as my Creator,
Redeemer, and heavenly Father, amen.*

"Ask and it will be given to you; seek and you will find; knock and the door will be opened to you."

MATTHEW 7:7

"Ask and it will be given to you; seek and you will find; knock and the door will be opened to you."

MATTHEW 7:7

*A*sk . . . Seek . . . Knock . . . Do you see a growing intensity in the person's prayers? Sometimes a respectful request is sufficient. Sometimes we need to pray with a bit more passion and intensity. And sometimes we need to be willing to make some noise and take action as we approach our heavenly Father.

Jesus encouraged his followers to pray specifically and with respect, perseverance, and passion. And Jesus reassured his followers that God will answer, that those who pray will receive, find, and have the door opened. After all, Jesus pointed out, not even a human father would give his child a stone if the boy asked for bread! So of course our heavenly Father will respond to our prayers, giving us what is in line with his will and best for us.

And if God answers with a no or "Wait" rather than a yes, we know that we still have the gift of his presence with us. And he is the best answer to prayer.

Lord, help me pray with perseverance yet trusting in your good and perfect will, amen.

The LORD is slow to anger, abounding in love and forgiving sin and rebellion. Yet he does not leave the guilty unpunished.

NUMBERS 14:18

We couldn't be more different from our Lord. We are impatient, and anger comes easily; God is slow to anger. We who sometimes have a hard time loving members of our families definitely struggle to love our enemies. God abounds in love, choosing to love the entire race of sinful, rebellious human beings. We hold grudges against people who have deliberately hurt us. But God consistently pardons our sins, accepting us because of the perfect sacrifice of his Son, Jesus Christ.

Looking only at these three traits, we can be grateful that God is Judge of our world. He has high and holy standards, yet he is loving and forgiving. Of course, he will be fair as he brings justice. People suffering under oppression, victimized by economic forces and the dictates of culture, or targeted by crime and terrorism can be confident that God will judge.

One day everything will be made right by our patient, loving, and forgiving God.

Lord, thank you that you are loving and forgiving and yet the perfect judge, amen.

What is your life? You are a mist that appears
for a little while and then vanishes.

JAMES 4:14

*L*ife's brevity is generally something we try not to think about and rarely talk about. But for the writers of the Bible—in this instance, James—the inevitability of our death is an important fact to remember. We need the reminder it offers that life is short; that we get only one shot at it; and that we can't go back and change things, no matter how desperately we wish we could.

We are a morning mist, a fading flower, a vapor. That should not scare us, but motivate us just as being told they have a handful of months to live motivates patients to live with intentionality. They spend time with people they love. They travel, go on mission trips, and write checks to favorite ministries. They resolve conflicts, apologizing and asking forgiveness, accepting apologies and granting forgiveness.

We don't know when our lives will end. But we can live as if each day were the last: we can live loving God and loving others.

Lord, help me to live with intentionality and use my time on this earth for your glory, amen.

*Do nothing out of selfish ambition
or vain conceit. Rather, in humility
value others above yourselves.*

PHILIPPIANS 2:3

The command to "value others above yourselves" goes completely against our basic human nature. Our bent is to look out only for ourselves, to spend our time pridefully satisfying self. But here Paul called us not only to be countercultural but to act in a way completely counter to our very nature.

How can we do this? What can we do to rid ourselves of the selfishness we are born with? We ask God to give us the heart and mind of Jesus Christ, to enable us to see people the way Jesus sees them and to serve them the way he served. Jesus let himself be interrupted and inconvenienced by others; he let go of his agenda for the sake of others.

We can be like Jesus only if we rely on the power of the Holy Spirit within us. He convicts us when we act out of selfishness, ambition, or conceit. He opens our eyes to the needy around us. He enables us to die to self.

*Lord, I want to die to self and honor
you by living for others, amen.*

I always thank my God as I
remember you in my prayers.

PHILEMON V. 4

In this short letter to Philemon, Paul and Timothy tell Philemon something we all like to hear: they are grateful for him, and they are praying for him. It's always nice to hear those two things from a friend or relative. So how about "doing unto others" today?

Who in your life could use some encouragement? Will you email, call, send a text, or handwrite a note telling them that you appreciate them and/or that you're praying for them? Everyone can benefit from hearing that!

When you do encourage your friends and family members, be specific about why you appreciate them. What has she done to inspire you in your faith? How has his faith after he lost his job encouraged you? What character traits are praiseworthy? What thoughtful gesture do you still remember? Write out a prayer—or leave a prayer in a voice mail.

Being specific about our appreciation and praying for someone we care about are gifts that nourish a heart.

Lord, please show me whom to
encourage today and who needs to
know I'm praying for them, amen.

"If you have faith as small as a mustard seed, you can say to this mountain, 'Move from here to there,' and it will move. Nothing will be impossible for you."

MATTHEW 17:20–21

*I*n our own strength, much that we might want to do in this life is impossible. But when we are walking through life with God, we step into his realm of miraculous possibilities. In fact, he thrives on doing the impossible. He wants us to learn to trust him for those big and seemingly impossible outcomes.

Thankfully, we don't have to have a mountain-sized faith to start. Big things (a twenty-foot mustard bush with a twenty-foot spread) happen from small beginnings (a one-millimeter-in-diameter mustard seed).

Clearly, planting that minuscule seed in the ground requires faith. The farmer had enough faith to bury it, then God caused the miracle of the tree.

Like the farmer, bury the tiny seed of your faith and entrust the outcome to Jesus.

Lord, you know that my faith feels small at times. I am so grateful that you can do big and even impossible things in response to that fleck of faith as I simply trust you, amen.

December

Show me the way I should go, for to you I entrust my life.

PSALM 143:8

Let the morning bring me word of your unfailing love, for I have put my trust in you. Show me the way I should go, for to you I entrust my life.

PSALM 143:8

There's something special—even sacred—about mornings. We sense that life starts afresh with the sunrise. What seemed impossible the night before now seems doable. And God's unfailing love dawns once again, renewing our hope, reminding us that we are loved.

To best experience God's love in the morning, we can make a habit of spending time listening for his voice. Maybe in the shower or on the drive to work you can allow yourself some quiet time to listen for his voice, review the truth of Scripture that you have memorized, or sing praise to your faithful God.

In that space of morning quiet before the bustle of the day begins, you will more easily hear God's promises to love you always and to guide you in the way you should go. Leave that morning quiet with him. Walk through the day together.

Lord, thank you for reminding me of your love every morning, making me confident in my choice to trust you, amen.

"I am the way and the truth and the life. No one comes to the Father except through me."

JOHN 14:6

Our world maintains that there are many avenues to God. Among them are following the teachings of Buddha, doing good deeds, achieving the level of enlightenment, and adhering to certain ascetic religious practices. And the world is wrong. The absolutely only way to the one true God is knowing Jesus as Savior and Lord. Belief in Jesus is the only way we can approach the Father, enter into relationship with him, and live in his love.

We don't have to try to impress God with our goodness or jump through religious hoops to please him. There's nothing—*nothing*—we can do, no lifestyle plan we can follow, no specific discipline to practice to be able to approach God. Again, simply believe that Jesus Christ paid the price for your sin once and for all. Your salvation is a gift. Go ahead and rest in your Father's embrace.

Lord, thank you that I don't have to earn my salvation and that it is secure because of Jesus' death on the cross for my sin, amen.

THE
ALMIGHTY
WILL BE
YOUR
GOLD,
THE
CHOICEST
SILVER
FOR
YOU.
JOB
22:25

December 3

The Almighty will be your gold,
the choicest silver for you.

JOB 22:25

Job was the righteous man whom God allowed Satan to sift. Job lost his family, his wealth, and his health when God gave Satan permission to take them away.

In light of these losses, Eliphaz the Temanite urged Job to "submit to God and be at peace with him" (v. 21). Those words must not have been easy for Job to hear in light of his desperate situation. Yet this advice has merit: we cannot see God as being more valuable than possessions, wealth, health, or family *until* we submit to him.

This world offers lots of flash and hype, so we too easily buy into the notion that financial security will bring peace. That's a complete deception. Ultimately, only God provides security.

Can you truly say God is more important to you than the blessings he provides? Do you value him more than his gifts? Doing so brings incredible freedom and peace.

Lord, I want to live with you being more important than anything I have or want. Please work in my heart, that I may value you more than the shiny things this world offers, amen.

Blessed is the one who perseveres under trial because, having stood the test, that person will receive the crown of life that the Lord has promised to those who love him.

JAMES 1:12

This reward—the crown of life—marks the culmination of a demanding race, the course marked by trials, pain, the desire to give up, wily schemes of the devil, and spiritual, emotional, and even physical exhaustion. Still, you persevere. You may run with a limp—or a hip joint may be out of place. Your knees may ache, and you may be gasping for breath. Sometimes all you can do is put one reluctant foot in front of the other.

Yet you persevere, and the reward erases every thought of the pain. The reward is eternal life with its abundant blessings of—among many—a new body, no more tears, and face-to-face communion with Jesus.

So persevere. Take the next step. Endure. Draw strength from your Lord. Rely on his Spirit within you. Keep your eyes on heaven. And keep in mind your heavenly Father's great love.

Lord, persevering is hard. You know the trials I face, and you know I keep putting one foot in front of the other for you, amen.

"'He will wipe every tear from their eyes. There will be no more death' or mourning or crying or pain, for the old order of things has passed away."

REVELATION 21:4

As our physical bodies become less comfortable and less able, we groan for redemption. As we age, we also experience more and more heartache. After decades on this sin-filled planet, we long for everything to be made right, for our suffering to make sense, and for us to be reunited with those who have gone before us to heaven. We have these yearnings according to the design of our Creator God.

God created us for himself; he created us to be in relationship with him. By his Spirit, he walks with us every step we take, he feels our every heartache, and he experiences with us every loss that comes. His compassion sustains us, as does the truth that in heaven we will look into Jesus' face and see in his eyes his great love for us. The anguish of life will slough off. We will know the joy of heaven where crying and pain will no longer exist. Come quickly, Lord.

Lord, I'm so grateful that I'll be whole someday, amen.

For the love of money is a root of all kinds of evil. Some people, eager for money, have wandered from the faith and pierced themselves with many griefs.

1 TIMOTHY 6:10

*M*oney is the root of all evil" is a popular misquote of this verse. Paul wrote that the *love* of money spawns evil. As he explained, money can subtly but effectively distract us. We can find ourselves wandering away from God.

What is money's attraction? It is manifold. Money means power and prestige. It can mean influence and status. It establishes a pecking order, provides a false sense of self-worth, and offers a deceptive sense of security. Money can reshuffle our priorities, turn our eyes from God, and pierce us "with many griefs."

God did not intend money to overshadow the value we have in his eyes or to distract us from the unshakable and eternal security he provides. God gave us money as a tool by which we can, for instance, love him by supporting his church and love others by helping to meet their needs.

Lord, help me to use the money you entrust to me to love you and love others. May I never love the money itself, amen.

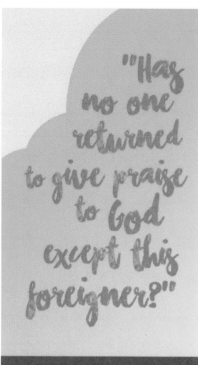

"Has no one returned to give praise to God except this foreigner?"

LUKE 17:18

Jesus healed ten lepers, Dr. Luke reported in his gospel account of the Savior's life. Jesus was nearing Samaria when the lepers shouted after him, asking him to have mercy on them. Who knows how long they had lived with this terrible condition, where nerves are so damaged that lepers no longer feel pain. And that inability to feel pain results in all sorts of injuries, and leper colonies were full of people who had lost fingers, toes, and even limbs. And, yes, lepers were forced to live apart from society with other lepers.

Jesus heard their cry for mercy and simply sent them to the priests for the requisite declaration of healing. As they went, all ten were healed, yet only one returned to thank Jesus. And he was a Samaritan, a half-breed Jew hated by Israel. No one thanked Jesus "except this foreigner."

This healed Samaritan shows us that everyone is included in Jesus' kingdom—and that those of us in the kingdom should live lives of gratitude.

Lord, you have healed me of much and blessed me with much. Thank you, amen.

The message of the cross is foolishness to those who are perishing, but to us who are being saved it is the power of God.

1 CORINTHIANS 1:18

To the world, the cross is foolishness—but, Paul explained, this apparent foolishness was planned by the God whose "foolishness" trumps man's greatest intelligence. God's ways may indeed appear foolhardy and strange, but they are ultimately the ways of salvation, eternal life, contentment, peace, and countless other blessings.

Still, the cross looks far more like foolishness than power. It doesn't make sense that a show of utter powerlessness and total defeat—a body hanging on a cross—actually set the stage for God's ultimate victory over sin and death. Jesus' resurrection ushered humanity into a relationship with God: this relationship that was once impossible because of sin was made possible by the sacrifice of sinless Jesus.

Jesus ransomed you from death row, and it cost him his life, which he allowed to be taken from him on the cross. Truly, the cross reveals the saving power of God.

Lord, some consider the cross sheer foolishness, but I know it as the means by which you graciously welcomed me into your eternal kingdom, amen.

How good and pleasant it is when
God's people live together in unity!

PSALM 133:1

*J*esus said that people will know that we follow him when they see the love we have for each other. The apostle Paul talked about the body of Christ and how important it is for believers to have connection, community, and unity. The author of Hebrews encouraged believers to gather together, encourage one another, and "spur one another on toward love and good deeds" (10:24). Peter encouraged believers to bear each other's burdens. And the apostle John wrote much about love, particularly loving other believers.

Clearly, love and unity are to characterize God's people. When we live in unity as the psalmist celebrated, we will experience good and pleasant times. Life is more peaceful when we choose unity and grace.

In what relationship do you need to choose unity and grace? In light of this verse, let go of bitterness. Ask for forgiveness if necessary; extend forgiveness if necessary. Be a person of reconciliation and know God's pleasure in you.

Lord, show me whom I need to reconcile with
—and give me the courage to do so, amen.

December 10

*The peace of God, which transcends all
understanding, will guard your hearts
and your minds in Christ Jesus.*

PHILIPPIANS 4:7

*A*t some level we think—wrongly—that
we can take care of ourselves, that we
can in our own power protect our hearts from
harm and our minds from corruption. All we
need to do is make the right decisions, develop
healthy habits, and have a contingency plan,
right? Paul said, "Wrong." We can't, by our own
willpower, protect our minds and hearts or
find the kind of peace God wants us to experience. The supernatural peace God has for us
defies explanation as we experience it in the
most unlikely situations, in the most painful
or stressful seasons of life, in the darkest or
stormiest of times, when we have no reason at
all to be at peace.

But when we approach God—which we
are able to do because of Jesus—and entrust
our lives to him, he will give us this peace that
sustains us. His peace also serves as a shield
protecting our hearts and minds against worries, fears, and doubts.

*Lord, thank you for your indescribable
peace and the protection it offers
my mind and my heart, amen.*

"I AM THE *light* OF THE WORLD."

JOHN 8:12

*"I am the light of the world. Whoever
follows me will never walk in darkness,
but will have the light of life."*

JOHN 8:12

We live in a dark world. Satan brings darkness wherever sin lurks. But Jesus said he is the Light of the World who came to dispel the darkness of Satan's lies and deceit as well as the ultimate darkness of sin and death. Darkness can't be wherever Jesus is.

That's why Jesus promised us that if we follow him, we will "never walk in darkness." We will have the light of truth in a world that claims various untruths as truth. We'll have the light of guidance when the world's voices call our name. We'll have light that brings healing and growth just as it does in the natural world. And we'll have the light of hope when this world beats us down.

The Light of the World will disperse the darkness within us and around us as we follow him.

*Lord, thank you that wherever I go, I
walk in the light of your truth, guidance,
healing, growth, and hope, amen.*

*Whatever is true, whatever is noble, whatever
is right, whatever is pure, whatever is lovely,
whatever is admirable—if anything is excellent
or praiseworthy—think about such things.*

PHILIPPIANS 4:8

To see more clearly what Paul was encouraging the Philippians to do, look at the opposite of the qualities he deems worth thinking about: True/false. Noble/dishonorable. Right/wrong. Pure/impure. Lovely/ugly. Admirable/detestable. Excellent/shoddy. Praiseworthy/worthless.

We should not tell lies, dishonor others, cheat, or indulge in impure thoughts, shows, or media. We should not rank sin, rationalizing that at least we're not as bad as _____ and giving ourselves permission to not repent. We should not endorse things that destroy God's creation. We should not do half-hearted work.

Now back to the positives and the truth that, left to ourselves, we cannot think only about what Paul listed. But calling on the Holy Spirit, we can. He will empower us to focus our minds and honor God with our thoughts. And the result will be greater peace.

*Lord, I want to fix my mind only on
excellent and praiseworthy things—
and I need your help, amen.*

"I am the bread of life."

JOHN 6:35

*"I am the bread of life. Whoever comes
to me will never go hungry, and whoever
believes in me will never be thirsty."*

JOHN 6:35

We have an insatiable thirst and desperate hunger that the world can never satisfy. Even when we fulfill a dream, or reach a goal, or find that relationship we've always wanted, we still find ourselves hungry and thirsty.

And here's why: God designed us to find our true and complete satisfaction in him. He designed us so that our appetites can be satiated only by him. If we pursue other things (even good things), we will finish the pursuit hungrier than when we started.

How do we escape this cycle of chasing after things that will never satisfy? We run instead to Jesus. He is the bread of life. He alone can satisfy and sustain our souls. He is the source of living water that completely quenches our thirst.

Are you hungry? Needy? Unfulfilled? Thirsty for something? The world doesn't have anything to help you. The answer is Jesus Christ. When you choose to follow after him, you'll finally know soul satisfaction and peace.

*Lord, forgive me for chasing things and people
that don't satisfy. I choose you today, amen.*

*I can do all this through him
who gives me strength.*

PHILIPPIANS 4:13

The apostle Paul had learned "the secret of being content in any and every situation . . . whether living in plenty or in want" (v. 12), and today's verse is that secret.

Relying on the Lord, we can be content no matter what we face. Whatever our circumstances, whether we're in a season of deprivation or abundance, God gives us his strength to endure, to choose to rest in him, and to experience contentment and perhaps even a touch of joy.

Notice that Paul didn't say we could find contentment in tough circumstances *in our own strength*. Contentment is a gift from the Lord. Only when we turn to Christ in humility, aware of our weakness and asking for his strength, will we be able to learn contentment. He may help us realize how blessed we actually are. He might open our hearts to the fact that we are rich in God's love and grace whatever our situation. And we can definitely know contentment in the blessing of Jesus' presence with us.

*Lord, you are the reason I can be content
anytime, anywhere, and I am grateful, amen.*

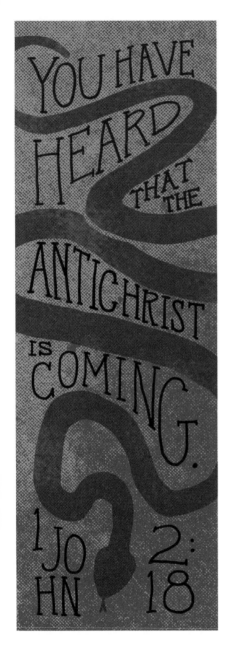

You have heard that the antichrist is coming.

1 JOHN 2:18

Throughout the Scriptures and especially in the New Testament, we are told about the end times and warned about the inevitable rise of the Antichrist. This leader will have the power of Satan and the ability to turn millions of people away from God. Jesus wants his followers to be ready for those days.

It's quite possible that the Antichrist could be alive today. But instead of worrying about it, instead of consulting charts and headlines, instead of trying to determine when Jesus will return as conquering King, we would be better off if we simply heeded Jesus' often repeated advice: be ready.

And we will be ready if we are living for Jesus; if, day by day, we love God with all we are, love the people in our lives, and honor Jesus in all we do. If we stay faithful to God like this, we won't be rattled by world events. Instead we'll rest in the peace and reassurance that come only from a strong relationship with Jesus.

Lord, I want to be prepared for the end times by loving you, loving people, and honoring you in all I do, amen.

*"The King will reply, 'Truly I tell you, whatever
you did for one of the least of these brothers
and sisters of mine, you did for me.'"*

MATTHEW 25:40

Jesus told his disciples a story about the end of the age when people will be separated into goats and sheep, and today's verse is the surprise ending. The goats, Jesus explained, had spent their lives ignoring people in need and doing nothing to help them. The sheep, however, had spent their lives feeding, clothing, nursing, and visiting people in need.

When these sheep acted kindly and with compassion, Jesus explained, they were actually showing him kindness and compassion. What a different perspective on what our ministry is all about!

Of course we aren't saved by doing good works, but those good works that result from our love for Jesus are more significant than you may have realized. When you choose to love that difficult relative or make a meal for a friend in need, it is as if you are doing so for Jesus himself.

*Lord, thank you for opportunities to serve.
What a privilege! Help me remember I am
serving you when I serve others, amen.*

*"This day I call the heavens and the
earth as witnesses against you that
I have set before you life and death,
blessings and curses. Now choose life, so
that you and your children may live."*

DEUTERONOMY 30:19

In the Old Testament, God offered rules that guided the daily lives of the Israelites. As Paul said, this law was given to make us conscious of our sin (Romans 3:20), of our inability to be holy and acceptable to our holy God. The people could obey or disobey. God's intention was always that his people would choose the path of life where love, not selfishness, motivated choices.

But individuals then—and since then and today—continually chose to act wickedly. As a result, the nation of Israel fell countless times. Israel simply could not do right. And neither can we.

Thankfully, God allowed Jesus' death on the cross—and his resurrection victory over sin—to pay the cost of our sins. We are forgiven, free to be in relationship with God, and empowered by his Spirit within us as we build the kingdom of God, an eternal kingdom of love.

*Lord, I can't do right. Thank you for sending
Jesus to take the punishment for my sin, amen.*

December 18

*In peace I will lie down and sleep, for you
alone, Lord, make me dwell in safety.*

PSALM 4:8

*J*n our world of chaos and pain, we can
find it hard to fall asleep at the end of
the day. Our minds spin with cares and worries, and we haven't always let go of the past.
We review regrets, missed opportunities, and
what we should've done. No wonder sleep
does not come easily some nights!

But today's verse reminds us of God's
great care for us, and he wants us to get a
good night's sleep. He wants to listen to our
anguished prayers. He wants us to give him
our burdens and worries. He cares about them
because we do, and he is far more capable of
carrying them and resolving them than we are.
And we can trust our faithful God to run the
world as we sleep.

God offers you peace and wants to bless
you with sleep every night as you lie down.
Instead of cataloging your worries in your
head, give them over to him tonight.

*Lord, I want to receive your gift of sleep,
so please take from me the worries
crowded in my head, amen.*

CLOTHE YOURSELVES
with
COMPASSION,
KINDNESS,
HUMILITY,
GENTLENESS,
and
PATIENCE.
COLOSSIANS
3:12

As God's chosen people, holy and dearly loved, clothe yourselves with compassion, kindness, humility, gentleness and patience.

COLOSSIANS 3:12

What we wear reflects who we are. And who we are is more about *whose* we are. Paul reminded us that we are chosen by God. For those of us who have felt like wallflowers in the dance of life, this is especially poignant news. The God of the universe has joyfully chosen you.

Not only that, but he calls you two very important things: "holy" and "dearly loved." *Holy* is a heady word. But your holiness is assured not because of what you've done or not done, but because of what Jesus did on the cross. And that same act on the cross—his death that paid the price for your sins—enabled you to become his dearly loved child.

In light of that reality, God wants you to wear clothes in keeping with your identity. You who are made holy, who are loved wildly, will naturally wear "compassion, kindness, humility, gentleness and patience." Those traits flow freely from who you now are.

Lord, thank you that I am made holy, that I'm dearly loved. Help me live in light of that today, amen.

December 20

In the beginning was the Word, and the Word
was with God, and the Word was God.

JOHN 1:1

Why does it matter that Jesus was *with* God in the beginning and that Jesus *is* God? This statement matters because it teaches that Jesus is one member of the Trinity, of the Father, Son, and Holy Spirit. It matters because Jesus, who saved us all from our sins, also took part in creating our world.

Jesus is called "the Word," which means he is God's message to all of us. He represents and communicates everything we need to know about God's heart. And as he walked the earth, Jesus showed us what it means to love others. Jesus gave us not only words to live by, but also a life to pattern ours after.

Now, if you ever wonder whether Jesus cares about you, whether he notices you as you struggle, consider this: he left the beauty of heaven in order to communicate to you his love. He is indeed the best Word you could ever hope for.

Jesus, thank you for being the Word,
for communicating so remarkably on
that cross your love for me, amen.

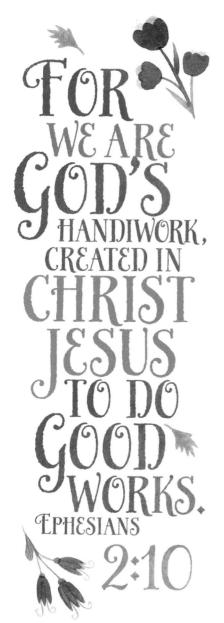

For we are God's handiwork, created in Christ Jesus to do good works, which God prepared in advance for us to do.

EPHESIANS 2:10

Imagine you've been asked to present at two different conferences. The first conference gives you no instructions. A typed note tells you where your presenting room is, but nothing more. At the second conference, a concierge greets you by name, gives you clear directions as to what you're to do, and hands you a packet of information about the organizer's hopes and goals.

Which experience would you prefer?

Like the concierge, God has anticipated your participation in his work in this world. He has, in fact, prepared "good works" for you to do. So he greets you today, warm and welcoming, and then, through the Holy Spirit, gives you clear directions. Also, in his written Word, the Bible, God shares his heart and outlines his hopes and goals for your life.

What an amazing truth! God has prepared in advance good works for you to do, and your doing them is important in his kingdom.

Lord, I'm grateful you've prepared good works for me today. Spirit, guide me to them and enable me to serve well, amen.

December 22

"My yoke is easy and my burden is light."

MATTHEW 11:30

*M*aybe you've noticed this, but something that's not particularly heavy can feel very heavy if we carry it too long. As Jesus addressed in this verse, he doesn't want us carrying around heavy things. So he invited people to find in him a specific kind of rest.

For too long the people of Israel had been yoked to the Pharisees' application of God's law. The Pharisees had done their best to clarify God's law in order to keep his people from violating the Ten Commandments. For too long the people had been burdened by the legalism.

Jesus wanted them to fling off that yoke and throw down those burdens and instead accept the forgiveness of sins he offered, the promise of eternal life, and the joy of living in God's grace today. Have you accepted Jesus' offer?

Know, too, that Jesus also cares about any and all situations, relationships, emotions, concerns, and demands that are making you weary. Go to him and find "rest for your souls" (v. 29).

Lord, thank you that I can give you all
my worries and burdens and receive
from you rest and peace, amen.

Let us then approach God's throne of grace with **CONFIDENCE.**

HEBREWS 4:16

Let us then approach God's throne of grace with confidence, so that we may receive mercy and find grace to help us in our time of need.

HEBREWS 4:16

In this verse, to be confident is to have the assurance that when we approach God, he will not yell at us or shake his finger our way. Many of us have experienced relationships with people who ruled with shame and ridicule, so much so that we feared approaching them.

Thankfully, God does not shame or ridicule. He sent his Son Jesus to die in our place, and he welcomes us wholeheartedly into his family. Our God is a good Father who unconditionally loves us and fully pardons us.

That's why the throne of our Father is called a throne of grace. It's a place where you are pardoned, reconciled, made new, and given a new path to walk. It's a place where, when you stumble, your heavenly Father gently dusts you off and encourages you to move forward. He doles out mercy aplenty, and he is not angry at your neediness.

Lord, I am very aware that I need you.
Please shower me with your grace, amen.

Let us run with perseverance the race marked out for us, fixing our eyes on Jesus, the pioneer and perfecter of faith. For the joy set before him he endured the cross, scorning its shame, and sat down at the right hand of the throne of God.

HEBREWS 12:1–2

*D*id you realize that joy compelled Jesus through the crucifixion? As this passage reminds us, Jesus foresaw joy, and that future picture helped him endure the greatest suffering known to man.

What was that future joy? It was the beautiful picture of forgiven humanity reconciled to a holy God because of Jesus' sacrificial death. Essentially, the joy was you and everyone else who calls on his name to be saved.

When Jesus uttered "It is finished" on the cross, he declared that he had accomplished God's will.

Having created the opportunity for you to be in relationship with God, Jesus can rightly be called the pioneer and the perfecter of your faith.

Lord, the only way I can thank you for enduring the cross, for being the initiator and the completer of my faith, is to honor you with my life. Please help me do so, amen.

And my God
will meet
all your
needs
according
to the
riches
of his
glory in
Christ
Jesus.

PHILIPPIANS 4:19

*And my God will meet all your needs according
to the riches of his glory in Christ Jesus.*

PHILIPPIANS 4:19

What a beautiful promise from God's Word! All our needs are met "according to the riches of his glory." But what exactly does that mean? What are "the riches of his glory"?

To determine that, we have to look at *doxa*, the Greek word for *glory*. In this context, *glory* means "honor, renown, and splendor." But it also means, in adjective form, "weighty, valuable, and worth much." The greatest value in this universe is God. He is weighty, worthy of everything. He is priceless.

So, you may have physical needs, and God attends to them. But there's so much more to the riches of God. Through the Holy Spirit, you have access to all of God, in the fullness of all his amazing attributes, in the fullness of his love, joy, peace, patience, kindness, goodness, faithfulness, gentleness, and self-control (see Galatians 5:22–23). He will gift you with his presence even as he meets all your needs.

*Lord, thank you that from your richness,
you so greatly enrich me, amen.*

December 26

The Spirit of God has made me; the breath of the Almighty gives me life.

JOB 33:4

*E*ven after all the trials Job encountered in his life, he still gave God glory for creating him. We would understand Job shaking an angry fist God's way and turning his back on the Almighty.

We would also understand if Job chose to simply conclude that God didn't exist. That reasoning can make sense of this capricious world where happenstance and tragedy seem to reign.

But Job chose to believe that God existed despite the loss and pain he had experienced. Job's great faith is an example for us when we face our own trials. Like Job, we are wise to believe that God is real, that he who created us is intimately acquainted with us, that our heavenly Father loves us, and that he will see us through the most difficult and painful circumstances.

Whatever trial you're facing today, whatever pitfalls and wrong turns and confusion, take a moment to quiet yourself. Remind yourself that God is big and that he promises to never leave or forsake you.

Lord, despite my feelings about my trials, I choose to believe that you love me, amen.

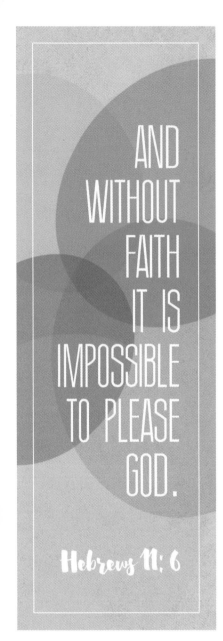

AND WITHOUT FAITH IT IS IMPOSSIBLE TO PLEASE GOD.

Hebrews 11: 6

And without faith it is impossible to please God.

HEBREWS 11:6

We desperately want to please God, right? So we try to be super-Christians and do mighty acts for him. Or maybe we embark on a self-imposed self-improvement program, hoping our efforts will merit his affection.

None of these efforts please God. Our attempts to earn his approval don't impress him. Why? Because as we rely on our own strength, we actually demonstrate we can live our lives without him.

What impresses God is your weakness—and not just your weakness, but your choice to turn to him when you're aware of your weakness. That's called faith. It's realizing you cannot do great spiritual acts in your own strength, and instead you fall on your knees and ask God to do what he does best in your weakness.

If you want to please God, simply ask him to intervene in your life wherever you are right now.

Act on your faith by simply talking to God, asking for his strength every moment, and trusting that he will provide.

Lord, thanks that faith isn't about something I do, but it's about whom I believe in. And thank you for calling me to believe in you, amen.

God did not send his Son into the
world to condemn the world, but to
save the world through him.

JOHN 3:17

Grace is hard to come by in the natural world these days. Perhaps you have experienced harsh judgment and haughty condemnation from all sorts of people who are "right."

Jesus had a different approach when he came to earth. His mission was to save the world, not condemn it. Jesus left heaven to mingle with us: he chose to dirty himself with our human limitations—and he lived the perfect, sin-free life that we can't. Furthermore, Jesus sought the outcasts, he healed lepers, he gave eyesight to the blind, he forgave people's sins—all this to show us God's grace.

And because of God's grace, you can go before him, confess your sin, be forgiven, and enjoy a relationship with him. Jesus allowed his shoulders to be weighed down with your sins so you could have access to God.

What a beautiful gift of grace!

Lord, I'm so grateful that you took my sin
upon yourself so I could experience your grace.
Help me to tell the people in my life about this
grace and invite them to receive it, amen.

Consider it pure joy, my brothers and sisters,
whenever you face trials of many kinds.

JAMES 1:2

Sound impossible? Notice how J. B. Phillips translated this verse: "When all kinds of trials and temptations crowd into your lives my brothers, don't resent them as intruders, but welcome them as friends!" James later shared that trials and temptations make us stronger; they can be the catalyst for deep spiritual growth.

When facing trials, you must keep the long view in mind. Think back on your life. When have you grown the most? The truth is, we grow through trials. That's why J. B. Phillips advised us to welcome them as friends.

Seeing trials as intruders can make us resentful. Instead, receive them as pathways to new life, perspective, and wisdom.

This doesn't mean you can't have emotions about your trials. Absolutely acknowledge the painful place you're in even as you ask God to enable you to welcome that trial as a companion.

Lord, help me to welcome each trial you allow
as a friend. Help me keep the long view in mind,
that you are using this trial to grow me, amen.

*"I am the Alpha and the Omega," says
the Lord God, "who is, and who was,
and who is to come, the Almighty."*

REVELATION 1:8

God exists outside of time even as he is the beginning and the end of all things. He is the One who started your story in the darkness of your mother's womb. And he is in the process of writing your story today. He knows how many hairs cover your head, the deepest worries of your heart, and the last day you'll walk on this earth.

Revelation 1:8 reminds us of God's vastness and power, yet he still chose you out of billions to live your amazing story on this earth. He is the mighty one who comes alongside you, gives you life, helps you forgive, and inaugurates hope.

What an amazing thought that your big God has such a tender heart for you. Focus on that truth especially if you are battling your own sense of worth today. Or hurting after someone's painful words. Or stressed about money. Know that the Almighty God loves you.

*Lord, you are the Alpha and the Omega,
the beginning and the end, yet you see
me and call me your child, amen.*

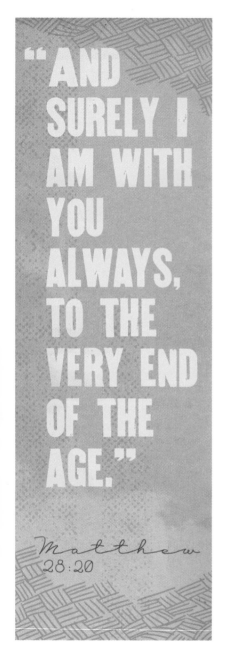

"AND SURELY I AM WITH YOU ALWAYS, TO THE VERY END OF THE AGE."

Matthew 28:20

*"And surely I am with you always,
to the very end of the age."*

MATTHEW 28:20

What words of comfort for his disciples whose world had been turned upside down!

The risen Jesus spoke these words to his disciples before he ascended into heaven. This promise was and is a solid rock of truth they could build their lives on just as you and I can. Then, on the Day of Pentecost, the disciples received the gift of the Holy Spirit and first experienced Jesus' new way of being present with them. As the disciples spread the good news, they did so in their Lord's strength.

Fast-forward over two thousand years. The Holy Spirit has continued to work through Christ followers who continued to share the gospel with others. And now this promise uttered to the disciples is spoken over you.

Think about that amazing promise: you are never alone, and Jesus will never leave you. That's true when you are sharing the gospel, but it's also true when troubles threaten to overwhelm. What a great promise from God!

*Lord, help me to realize afresh that you
are near and you won't leave me, amen.*